Uncommon Will

The Death and Life of Sue Rodriguez

Uncommon Will

The Death and Life of Sue Rodriguez

Lisa Hobbs Birnie

Sue Rodriguez

Macmillan Canada

Toronto

Canadian Cataloguing in Publication Data

Birnie, Lisa Hobbs, 1928-
    Uncommon will

ISBN 0-7715-9091-1

1. Rodriguez, Sue, 1950-1994.   2. Right to die—British Columbia.
3. Assisted suicide—British Columbia.   4. Amyotrophic lateral
sclerosis—Patients—British Columbia—Biography.   I. Title.

RC406.A24B57   1994   362.1'9683'092   C94-931398-X

Macmillan Canada wishes to thank the Canada Council, the Ontario Ministry of Culture and Communications and the Ontario Arts Council for supporting its publishing program.

Macmillan Canada
A Division of Canada Publishing Corporation
Toronto, Canada

1 2 3 4 5 FP 98 97 96 95 94

Printed in Canada

Acknowledgements

Lisa Hobbs Birnie gratefully acknowledges the contribution made by the following: Liz Campbell; Sue Ritchie; Helma Libick; Cilla Kotz; Margaret Mackay; Carol Fancy; the staff at the Vancouver Public Library; and most of all, Wilf Birnie.

Uncommon Will

One

Andrew Eisen, M.D., stood at the window of his modest, second-story office in the neuromuscular unit of Vancouver General Hospital vaguely watching the flow of traffic below, his mind on the patient in the examining room next door.

Her name was Susan Jane Rodriguez. She lived in Saanich, about 30 miles north of Victoria on Vancouver Island. A striking woman, thought Eisen, competent and bright. She'd turned 41 just two weeks earlier. If she made 44, she'd be lucky—if months of infantile helplessness preceding death could be called luck. He'd noticed on her chart she was separated from her husband and had a child. Poor mother, poor kid, and not a damn thing any-one in the world could do about it. He returned to his desk and waited while the patient dressed.

At 56, Dr. Eisen ranked among the leading neurologists specializing in amyotrophic lateral sclerosis in North America. Lou Gehrig's disease it was popularly called, after one of baseball's greatest players died from it. Eisen was born in Berlin, raised in England, received his degree in medicine at Leeds University. The walls of his office reflected his cosmopolitan background and status—years with the Neurological Institute in Montreal, tributes and

1

plaques from India, from Africa. None of this helped him now.

He dreaded the task at hand. Rodriguez had no idea of the nature of her illness, didn't realize she had *any* form of motor neuron disease, although tests in mid-June had shown it. After they'd finished the PET (positron emission tonography) scan on her brain a half hour ago and she was still lying on the examination table, he'd put his hand on hers and asked if anyone had told her about her diagnosis. Surely someone would have told her *something* by now! But she'd replied no, she didn't have any idea what was going on.

He'd never become used to telling people that they had a terminal disease, although God knows he'd had enough practice. He sometimes felt that people were better at receiving the news than he was at giving it. Many simply came out with it: "I've got ALS, haven't I?" He'd never become used to that either—the calm, the courage of ordinary people dealt such a terrible blow. But it didn't always work out like that. Some people simply couldn't grasp the fact that they were dying and nothing could be done about it, and others simply couldn't cope. Each time it was a judgment call.

For Dr. Eisen, there were always two questions with patients who were innocent of their impending, cruel death: "Will I tell them?" and "How quickly will I tell them?" On meeting Sue Rodriguez, he had decided almost instantly to tell her the truth.

She received the news in silence. Dr. Eisen didn't want to burden her with too much information—patients rarely took it in after such a shock anyway—but he wanted to be frank and clear. He said there was no known cause and no known cure. In some cases, perhaps ten percent, there appeared to be a hereditary element, but usually ALS struck at random. He told her she would experience progressive muscle atrophy resulting from loss of spinal and cortical motor neurons over months to years. This would lead to complete paralysis and eventual death.

He tried to be as positive as the wretched circumstances allowed: "You're very young. Who knows? There's tremendous work going on." He told her the rate of discovery and understanding about ALS has probably outmaneuvered every other disease and that the puzzle was unfolding as expediently as possible: "It may well be that we might be able to treat ALS and never understand its cause and mechanism. In terms of the future we *must* be very positive."

Still she sat looking at him and saying nothing. He told her that the ALS Clinic of B.C. was testing a drug called Lamotrigene to see if it would slow down the ALS process. Maybe after she'd thought about it, she might like to become involved in the program. She inclined her head as if to say she didn't know, but said nothing.

Recalling this meeting a year later in a television interview, she would speak of "Dr. Eisen's coldness" and "insensitivity" toward her. Even on this day, August 22, 1991, at Vancouver General Hospital, Dr. Eisen could sense she was angry. Against fate? Against him? Maybe he'd called the wrong shot, should have gone about telling her differently. He had devoted his life to working on this deadly disease to help, not hurt, its victims. But was there really a good way to tell someone they're going to die? So he said: "Look, there's a lot you have to think about and be concerned about. We need to talk this over in the ensuing days and weeks."

Walking down the hall away from his office, Sue Rodriguez felt her knees buckle, her legs turn to water. She knew what ALS was, had seen the documentary on physicist-astronomer Stephen Hawking, knew his condition, tried to imagine her own life inside a body that couldn't sit up, walk, talk, laugh, write or hug her child. Then the realization broke over her. She would never see her son Cole grow into a teenager, never know him as a man. She leaned against the wall. She became aware of a terrible sound, as primal as the cry of a wounded animal, unlike anything she'd heard before. She realized only slowly, from the horrified expressions of passersby, that it was coming from her own mouth.

She'd stayed the night before at the University of British Columbia (UBC) campus University Hospital, and the ambulance attendant who'd been waiting to take her back there came running at the sound. He helped her to the ambulance, and stayed with her, chatting softly and senselessly about cures while they were driving to UBC. His was the only kindness she felt that day. The neurologist and other medical staff on the campus site knew of the ALS diagnosis, and on her return to her wing, she sensed their awkwardness and embarrassment. Not one doctor or nurse spoke to her, held her, attempted to comfort her. She phoned to tell her mother and stepfather, Doe and Ken Thatcher. Doe said: "Ken and I thought it might be that." Sue felt abandoned, and gave way to uncontrollable grief.

When she was calmer, she telephoned Dr. Sandra Elder, a professional grief counselor in Victoria who had helped her when she and her husband, Henry, had separated six months earlier. Henry was caring for Cole while Sue was in Vancouver. She asked Dr. Elder to tell Henry about the diagnosis so that their seven-year-old son would not witness a painful emotional scene when she arrived home.

It struck her there was no point to her staying on at the centre. There was nothing anyone or any hospital could do. No more tests and no more uncertainty. She told a staff doctor she was leaving, and the inevitability of her fate was confirmed by his indifference. No one attempted to stop her, no one seemed aware that the death sentence she had just received might put her safety at risk. Alone, she packed her bags, went to the campus lot where she'd parked her Volvo and drove to the ferry terminal at Tsawwassen. Later, she would have no recollection of the drive through the heavy late-summer traffic, or where she went, or how she got there.

The journey from Tsawwassen to Vancouver Island takes an hour and thirty-five minutes. Standing on the deck, leaning against the railing as the ferry glided along the timbered shoreline and through the passages of the Gulf Islands, she realized with some surprise that she felt nothing. She couldn't think about the future, about her illness, about life or death. Only the stunning, ungraspable fact that she would be leaving Cole for others to raise and love.

Sue would die two and a half years later, the pain of leaving her child unmitigated. But the journey into a helpless and anonymous oblivion, which she anticipated the day of her diagnosis, would never occur. Paradoxically, in the process of dying, she would metamorphose into a powerful warrior. Inner gifts of which she knew nothing would surge into life as her muscles atrophied. Her voice, weakened into a dragging, slurring monotone, would become a cry for justice, her wasted body a symbol of strength. Deciding on a physician-assisted suicide, she would take her battle to the Supreme Court of Canada. She would become an international figure, loved, hated, praised and pitied by some of society's most powerful cultural, moral and ethical institutions.

This transformation would not turn Sue Rodriguez into a saint. She would remain bitter toward her husband, distant with many of her family. Unable or unwilling to use her newfound strengths to change attitudes and habits that had marked her character since childhood, she would destroy many of her own dreams and create for herself profound psychological pain. To the end, her belief in the correctness of her own standards would remain inflexible, her need to control, profound. Yet the grace and strength that she would project, the calm dignity that would make the sweet face of Sue Rodriguez instantly and nationally recognizable, would not be an illusion or a staged image. Her serenity would mirror other positive facets of a personality whose very complexity was the fulcrum of all her strengths.

As she drove off the ferry on that late-August day, her sole thought was to reach the familiarity and security of her own home—tenuous though it was. There was no thought of tomorrow or the days ahead. She parked on the

driveway outside the double garage and went through .
front door. Henry stood there with Cole. Behind them she
could see the table set for dinner that Henry, unbidden,
had prepared. She burst into tears. He opened his arms
and embraced her.

February to August 1991

The knowledge that her body would betray her, that it had its own life and secrets independent of her will and was, in fact, already on a return journey to infantile dependency and premature death, came as the final blow at the end of a summer that was marked by confusion and loss.

The unraveling of Sue Rodriguez's life began one wet and chilly night in mid-February when Henry arrived home, said that the marriage was not working for him and announced that it was over. Soon after he left the home they'd bought three years earlier and moved into a rented apartment in downtown Sidney.

The marriage of Sue and Henry, a conventional couple with conventional dreams, had been heading toward a breakup for some time. Silent tension had given way to embarrassing outbursts of barbed hostility. The marriage had never worked particularly well. They had met at the University of California in San Diego where Henry had graduated in biochemistry. Sue had already been married once by then. She had married Bob Hendricks, a tool and die mechanic, when she was 21. They separated two years later and were divorced in 1975. In February 1976, Sue, who had frequently vacationed in California, settled in San Diego and joined a secretarial pool at the university.

In 1978, while working in the chemistry department, she met Henry. Sue was 28, divorced and dazzlingly attractive; Henry was 23, single and deeply shy.

He and Sue lived together for two years in San Diego. When his work took him to live in San Francisco in 1981, he knew the relationship should end, but he did not like being alone and missed Sue's companionship. He said Sue agreed to join him only if he married her, so he did. It was a mistake from the start. Henry later said that he was lonely and young when he married Sue, and although there was attraction and affection, it wasn't the stuff lasting marriages are made of. For her part, Sue would say it was true Henry could not stand being alone, nor did he like making difficult decisions. He was the only son of strong parents who'd made most of his major decisions for him. He liked Sue's strength, was comfortable with her decisiveness and needed the love she gave him. With time, Sue said, he had come to rebel against the very characteristics he'd once found so desirable.

Whatever the history, the marital relationship between Sue and Henry Rodriguez was over by the end of February 1991. Sue lived with Cole in the house on Cromarty Avenue in Saanich; Henry lived in his own apartment in Sidney. They had negotiated a separation agreement. They maintained fairly close contact, however, not only because of their child, whom they both adored, but because they were anxious to remain "best friends." Time would show that this ideal was not merely an attempt to look civilized, but that a powerful attraction—suffused with ambivalence—still existed between them. But there was no love, and because they'd been husband and wife and the separation had been fraught, it was naive to imagine they could be "best friends." In the years remaining, this malformed ideal would endure all contrary realities and create endless pain for both of them.

The first symptoms of Sue's illness asserted themselves in April. They were trivial enough. No pain, no numbness, just a tendency for her hands to twitch. Sometimes the little finger of her left hand would move away from her ring finger. Who would suspect a death sentence in something as simple as that?

Sue's living habits helped keep suspicion of any real health problem at bay. Her long limbs—she was five foot eight, 135 pounds—were slim and strong, the result of years of cross-country skiing and rock climbing. A decade earlier, when she lived in California, she'd run in a 13-mile marathon. Although she'd done with stretching herself too harshly, the disciplined habits remained. She walked a lot, didn't smoke, ate a high-fiber, low-fat diet, rarely drank more than a glass or two of white wine. As an administrator in a real estate office in downtown Victoria, she found her work stress-free and reasonably satisfying. Hers was a healthy life-style, the type that generates a sense of control over one's fate and pays small heed to mysteries like random mutations.

When the twitching in her hands continued, Sue checked in with Corrie Cowan, her family doctor, who referred her to a neurologist. She told Henry during one of their occasional meals in his apartment that it was probably tennis elbow or some sort of muscle stress caused by years of working on a computer. From Sue's viewpoint—

and as it turned out from the neurologist's—it was simply a matter of pinpointing the problem and fixing it.

Fixing it was a high priority with Sue because she was out of a job. Not long after Henry had walked out, the real estate company for which she worked went bankrupt. When he left the marriage, Henry had assumed a major share of the running expenses of their Saanich home with its nine rooms and acre of treed and landscaped grounds. The house was completely paid for, but Henry was in the process of forming his own biotechnology company, and he could not afford to increase the $900 per month. Bereft of any regular income beyond unemployment insurance and Henry's stipend, and hunting for a job in a down market, Sue decided to sell the house and find more modest accommodations for herself and her son. Henry agreed. Cole would probably have to switch schools, something neither of them wanted, but they decided they would cross that bridge when they came to it.

These were the circumstances of Sue Rodriguez's life when she made her first visit to a neurologist. The specialist noted Sue's complaints that her hands twitched, and that her little finger on the left hand would move away from the ring finger quite involuntarily. He also noted a sensation of tightness in her left arm and complaints of past spinal pain in her neck and lower back. There had been no headaches or dizziness, however, and her respiratory and cardiovascular systems were normal. Motor conduction also seemed normal. However, her mental status and cranial nerve examinations showed some anxiety.

After the examination was over, with no conclusions

drawn or suspicions aroused, the specialist and Sue sat down to talk. She mentioned that her ten-year marriage had recently broken down and that she was job hunting. On her departure he dictated a letter to Sue's family physician, Corrie Cowan. The patient, he said, was normal. The twitchings were probably "benign fasciculations" which tended to occur when people were under either physical or emotional stress, which she apparently was. With time they would subside spontaneously.

With the confidence that comes with a clean bill of health, Sue set about creating her new life. She joined Divorce Lifeline, a support group of erstwhile spouses working through the trauma of divorce, and started attending weekly meetings. She made a series of appointments with Dr. Sandra Elder (who had been Henry's counselor before the breakup) for counseling and guidance—a contact that would continue until Sue's death. She cleaned out her well-tailored, expensive wardrobe and held a garage sale, even though with no mortgage and Henry's quite sufficient contribution, she didn't really need the money. She liked living a certain way, she wanted to be independent and in control. Making it on her own was what really counted.

Sue, to all appearances, had accepted the end of her marriage. All her energies seemed to be directed towards creating her own life. But her sadness at her overall situation, and the ambivalence of her emotions regarding Henry's defection are reflected in a diary entry on the day of the garage sale, Sunday, April 28, 1991: "Today I feel many emotions—mostly sad. I'm tired after the garage sale and a very hectic weekend. I feel drained but am realizing the impact of Henry's message on Friday. He is not coming back. It is all very real. It's over."

Realizing at last that Henry was not playing games, that he wanted out and would never return, Sue searched for a smaller house and sent out dozens of résumés. By the second week of June, she still had no bites on the house but she did have three job possibilities. None was great. She'd had varied and challenging jobs in the past. Once she'd been a cross-country ski instructor in an extension program at the University of California at San Diego; at another time, she'd been coordinator of international and social events at Hanna House, Frank Lloyd Wright's historic residence at Stanford University, Palo Alto, California. But work was never the focus of her life. During her 12 carefree years in California, her passions had been skiing in the Sierras, photography courses, rock climbing, love affairs (and Henry) and white wine; she had not been a career woman. And her education was relatively limited. Ultimately, she could claim only two years of college, at Seneca in Toronto, and that was in early childhood education.

After some weeks and two interviews, she obtained work as a legal secretary. She was almost out of money. The job wouldn't be available until August; in the meantime she was to do a WordPerfect course which her new employers would pay for.

The summer was moving along painfully and slowly. Despite her uncertainty as to whether she wanted Henry back, and her anger at him for walking out, Sue found the house a sad and empty place without him. On those weekends when Cole went to his father, and she found herself left alone, the loneliness was almost unbearable. The Divorce Lifeline program helped a bit, but the group often met across town, she had to arrange for a baby-sitter, and when she got there found she couldn't open up the way the others could. She asked Henry to go but he refused. He was already going to his own counselor and did not feel that at that stage it would work with both of them going together.

With the house on the market, people were in and out and that meant constantly keeping it up. Then there was the roof. Since it had leaked in the chimney area during the winter, it had to be fixed and the insurance claim settled. Cole was in the Beavers, she was the treasurer of the troop, so there were meetings to attend. And there was Cole's birthday party: a sleep-over for ten little boys had been arranged for early June. But here Henry did almost everything. He decorated the entire house, cooked the barbecue, took the boys to the beach.

Small wonder that the sporadic, irritating twitching in her hands seemed to be getting worse. And to top off the worst months of her life, an old ache in her left shoulder, which she'd dislocated years earlier, had returned. Regular sessions with her chiropractor, Richard Elder (Dr. Sandra Elder's husband) didn't give any relief, and for the first time it struck Sue that maybe stress wasn't the cause, that the original diagnosis had perhaps been wrong. Once again she checked with Dr. Cowan, who this time ordered a spinal scan in the medical imaging department of the local hospital.

The results suggested that the first neurologist had been right. There were no visible abnormalities, the report stated. The word "visible" struck Sue. Was there a possibility of invisible abnormalities? She had always accepted responsibility for her health. Listening to her body's subtle signals was an ingrained habit. And so was questioning the opinion of others. The first neurologist had seemed sure the twitching would disappear. But it had not. And now there were other, almost indefinable, sensations. Every now and again her left arm felt different, weak, as if the twitches in her hand were spreading up it. And there was a tightness in her left foot, a peculiar sensation of a type not experienced before.

Sue became convinced that whatever the doctors had said and the tests shown, something was wrong. At her insistence, an appointment with a second neurologist was set up for mid-June. Meanwhile, her other problems didn't let up. In the three months the house had been on the market, they'd had only one serious offer. They'd accepted it but at the last moment the deal fell through. Since then not a bite. Sue felt she couldn't start earning a regular income soon enough and it was with relief that, in mid-June, she started her WordPerfect course. Shortly thereafter, she was examined by the second neurologist.

He said little as he probed and questioned. This silence and the vagueness and brevity of his responses aroused in Sue her first real apprehension. It was as if he'd caught a glimpse of something he didn't wish to share, something he saw no reason yet to impose on her. When she pushed for answers, he said that further tests were needed. But Sue, powerfully aware that it was her body they were dealing with, not his, wanted more. He replied that an

MRI scan (magnetic resonance imaging) would be the best way to determine what, if anything, was wrong and he'd set it up and be in touch. Sue felt he was brusque, dismissive.

When Sue left, the neurologist wrote to Dr. Cowan, describing Sue as an "alert, very pleasant lady" and giving the tentative diagnosis he had refused to share with her: "The problem is probably anterior Horn cell disease. Unfortunately, this most likely is going to turn out to be a variant of motor neuron disease. The investigation of choice, and most definitive procedure is MRI scan. I believe this should be done as an urgent procedure."

Two weeks later, Sue returned to his office, having learned that an MRI can take from four to six months to set up. It wasn't good enough, she told him. She'd go south, to Bellingham, Washington, and have it done there at her own expense if necessary. He retorted that there was no hurry. He then spoke about several families he'd known who had spent all their money getting the diagnosis of an illness for which nothing could be done. People often spent money uselessly, he said. Better they kept it for college or retirement. The specialist's attitude surprised and troubled Sue. She thought it bizarre. She was convinced by now that she had a nerve pressing on the vertebrae and couldn't understand why the doctor seemed to think it was useless for her to pursue it.

Sue felt pulled in a dozen directions. Summer was at its height. Since winter, she'd been living in emotional pain and financial uncertainty. She hankered for some peace and normalcy. From time to time she still had dinner with Henry. She was devastated to learn he'd started dating other women. Neighborhood parties, sometimes elegant indoor affairs, sometimes barbecues under the firs and pines that dotted each one of their well laid-out properties, had been something she'd loved in the past. Now she felt the odd one out, the only single person among the successful, happy couples. She had a contempt for self-pity, tried to control the feeling, but couldn't. The knowledge that Henry was dating other women fed it. It had become imperative that she establish her own life for herself and Cole independent of others.

Getting control over the silly twitches and pains had to be the first step, and in this respect she'd accomplished one thing. She had gone to yet another doctor, a general practitioner, and he'd advised her to act aggressively, to not waste any more time but to seek tests in Vancouver. She promptly scheduled an appointment for a series of tests at the UBC campus University Hospital for the third week in August.

One week before she was to go, Sue started her new job. It was a disaster. She needed the income and the independence that came with it, and was sensitive to the money spent on her WordPerfect training. But after two days it became clear she couldn't physically cope. The pain in her arms and hands had suddenly taken on a life of its own. She found a naturopathic doctor close to the office and spent every lunchtime seeking his help. She held on until Friday and then quit.

During that week, she had a strange, disconcerting experience. She had dressed for work and was staring closely into the mirror finishing her makeup. Suddenly she caught herself looking into her own eyes. They were familiar, yet strange. The face was hers, yet different. It was as if she had subtly changed, as if a stranger was slowly emerging from deep inside her body. She knew at that moment that something serious was happening to her.

The following week, Dr. Andrew Eisen told her what it was.

Three

As a child, Sue Rodriguez seemed to have been born under a lucky star. Her father, Tom Shipley, was one of four children of Howard and Virginia Shipley of West Hill, Virginia. Howard Shipley was a wealthy man whose holdings included the Canadian Ice Machine Company, a refrigeration and air-conditioning supplier located in Toronto. The Shipleys—the descendants of Adam Shipley of Yorkshire, England, who landed in Annapolis, Maryland in 1668—are one of America's founding families, a fact of which Sue was deeply proud. Sue's mother, Dorothea Gosnell, Doe as she is called, was the youngest of three daughters of an executive with the Rochester Gas and Electric Company and his well-educated, well-connected wife. They lived in Rochester, New York, and were considered comfortably off and socially well placed.

Grandparents Howard and Virginia (Gigi) had a summer cottage at Jack's Lake, Ontario, and purchased property for each of their four children nearby, but across the lake. Howard and Gigi also owned a hobby farm at West-hill, Ontario, staffed by a housekeeper and gardener. Later they acquired two homes near Puerto Vallarta, Mexico. One, Casa Gigi, a comfortable tropical cottage, was on the beach, and the other, far more substantial, Casa Zaragoza, was in Gringo Gulch, an area outside of Puerto Vallarta frequented by Americans.

Sue, the second child in a family of five children born within a ten-year span, spent much of her childhood around her paternal grandparents and was deeply influenced by them. Grandfather Howard, known by his initials "H.V.," was a product of the aristocratic Virginia Military Institute, and he acted and looked the part. He owned four cars, his personal preference being a black Cadillac. He was genial and popular with his colleagues, indulgent with his wife, Gigi—who preferred the pastel-colored T-Bird—and critical and controlling of his family. His one visible soft spot apart from Gigi was his spunky, long-limbed granddaughter, Sue.

Said Sue: "I loved my grandfather. There was nobody like him. I was the only one who could see through his facade. He had a very sweet side which he didn't show to everyone. Tom, my brother, was very close to him too and both of us kept in touch with him regularly to the end. I valued him, although he was a hard one to understand and I don't accept the way he treated his own family."

Gigi was an elegant, articulate and slightly eccentric woman who lived life to the hilt. She favored pink Italian suits and large diamonds, traveled widely abroad with and without her husband and dabbled in painting, writing and exotic cooking. If she didn't always do what her husband wanted, at least she made sure it appeared as though she did. Driving around the streets of Puerto Vallarta in her dune buggy, her braided gray hair woven around her head and entwined with ribbons, her suit white and her skin tanned, Gigi was, to young Sue's eye, the epitome of life and style.

Said Sue: "She was my mentor, teaching me the importance of reading, of grooming myself physically and mentally. She was an inspirational person for me, very clever, in control but she had to do it cleverly. When grandfather criticized his own children, she took part in it, she sided with him."

The entire scene was considerably less inspirational to Sue's mother, Doe, in those days a true beauty. Time has faded her looks, but her charm—that elusive, usually feminine ability not only to put others completely at ease but almost to enchant them—remains undiminished. Her husband, Tom, worked for grandfather Howard at the Canadian Ice Machine Company, as did Tom's brother, Peter. Both sons were expected to. They were given no choice. Tom and Doe and their children—Barbara, Susan, Thomas, Anne and Sarah (Sally)—lived in a suburban Toronto bungalow. Tom's salary was average; there were no perks. The "perks" that did come were contingent on compliance to Howard's will. Gigi and Howard's four children did not own, but simply used, the summer cottages "given" to each of them at Jack's Lake. At Howard and Gigi's pleasure, they bestowed educational benefits on their grandchildren.

Sue and her sisters were given a variety of "extras"—expensive summer camps, dancing lessons, piano lessons. Sue said that these extras, and the annual trek to the family's lakeside compound to spend summer with her own large clan, added to a feeling that she already had—that of being different and somehow "special." Anne and

Sally were sent to Havergal College, a private girls' school in Toronto. Sue, who had become a rebellious teenager—her parents were aghast to find her experimenting with marijuana—was sent to a Mennonite school in Niagara-on-the-Lake in the hope she'd stay out of trouble and develop better study habits. This was a move that her grandparents financed and that she resented to her dying day. "It turned out there wasn't room for me to live at the school so I was boarded out with a private family," said Sue. "Their living style was not at all what I was used to. I spent my entire time begging my parents to let me come home."

She lasted there less than a year. Soon after, at 16, grandfather Howard sent her off with a high school group for a summer study tour of Europe. When it came time for young Tom to go to the University of New Brunswick, H.V. once again lent a financial hand.

Doe endured these years with their incongruous mix of family wealth and personal powerlessness feeling resentful and demeaned by the manner in with Howard and Gigi controlled their adult children. Romantic and non-aggressive by nature, Doe understood that her husband was no match for his powerful father and was incapable of breaking loose from his dominance. This did nothing to allay her resentment, however, especially when Tom started to drink heavily. Today, widowed after a second, and extremely happy, marriage, Doe smiles when speaking of those times. But the smile is a matter of manners; it doesn't stop tears from filling her eyes.

"It was horrible," she says quietly. "Tom was belittled and I was powerless. His parents controlled their entire family with their money. They'd cut us out of the will if we didn't do this, or wouldn't do that. Tom's father was a tyrant, a bitter man, very conscious of his money. Sue saw a different side, her relationship was special. She loved him."

Doe recalled an incident that epitomized the family dynamics. It was Sue's 13th birthday, August 2, 1963, and the entire clan and as usual was gathered at Jack's Lake. Tom had organized a local regatta, had had a few drinks and had returned home late to find Sue and young Tom still running around outside in the hot, still summer air. He'd been angry, scolded them and sent them to bed. Instead of obeying, Sue and her brother rowed across the lake to their grandparents'. In that childish act lay a clear acknowledgment of who ruled that particular roost. Gigi and Howard kept the children, despite Doe's protests, and returned to Toronto with them. Two weeks passed before, as Doe put it, "they grew tired of having them around and returned them to us."

Sue gives a slightly different version of this incident, whose vivid remembrance down the years reveals its significance: "We'd hidden in the bushes. I didn't know what I'd done wrong when father scolded me. My feelings were hurt. It was my birthday and I'd gotten no attention because of the regatta. So we rowed over to my grandparents. That started a quarrel between my parents and grandparents and it was decided we'd stay."

Within the space of a few years, the Shipley clan suffered a series of profoundly tragic events. In the winter following the above incident, Howard and Gigi's 36-year-old daughter, Virginia, and three of her four children, died in a house fire. Virginia's husband, Phillip, was away on business. The curtains caught on a heater, the occupants were sleeping, the house exploded. One grandchild, Anna, whose second-floor bedroom had an outside balcony, survived. Five years later, Howard and Gigi's son, Tom, Sue's father, who had become an alcoholic, died of cirrhosis of the liver. He was 45. Not long after that, Howard and Gigi's youngest daughter, Elizabeth, died suddenly of a brain aneurysm. Elizabeth was in her early thirties.

At Tom's death, Howard Shipley established a trust fund for Tom's children and allotted an allowance of $800 a month to Doe, to continue until such time as she might remarry. The trust fund gave Sue a small private income for several years.

By the time Howard and Gigi reached their seventies, they had lost all their children but one, Peter. The family was further fragmented when Peter's marriage ended in a bitter divorce. Breaking free at last, he quit his father's business, took off for Greenwich Village and opened a vegetarian restaurant. He later remarried and moved to Mexico, where he died recently.

Next, aging and suffering from severe arthritis, Howard Shipley had to face the death of Gigi. He sold his Canadian properties, and accompanied by the elderly nurse who looked after him, moved to Charleston, South Carolina. He married this nurse, who'd been a Mennonite missionary in India, and died two years later. At his death, Howard Shipley left the remainder of his estate to his alma mater, the Virginia Military Institute.

Some time later, Sue visited her stepgrandmother. She

was stunned to find her not only wearing Gigi's clothes and jewelry, but dressing her hair in an identical manner. Sue thought the woman's attempts to be like the stylish Gigi were pathetic yet somehow touching. With time she developed a friendly, if casual, relationship with the elderly woman. One year Sue's Christmas present to her stepgrandmother was returned by United Parcel, the outside stamped "Addressee Deceased." Months passed before she felt like opening it. Then she removed the contents—wind chimes—and hung them on her own back porch, taking them with her whenever she moved house. Sue said that the return of the package marked the end of an era for her. The delicate, bell-like tinkling of the chimes was audible from the bedroom in which Sue finally chose to die.

It was in this setting of powerful intergenerational tensions, patriarchal control, upper-class family social rituals and conventional cultural values that Sue was raised. She thought her childhood and most of her adolescence a happy, carefree and privileged time. She shared the personal tragedies of the family generation that preceded her, but at a distance and with a certain fascination. She felt special in this larger-than-life family, and although the deaths of her aunts were real and painful, they were not traumatic.

Sue's loss of her father when she was 17 was another matter. While her memory of her grandfather remained vivid and powerful, that of her father seemed gray and tenuous. She felt his death, but it was memories of his illness that preceded it and the embarrassment of everyone's staring at her at his funeral, that was repeatedly recalled. Tom, his liver destroyed, was sick for a year, weak, wasted and dependent. It is worth noting that as he grew sicker, he moved out of his own home and returned to his mother, Gigi, to be nursed by her and to die. Asked why her husband didn't stay with his own family, Doe gave two reasons: "to spare his family suffering," and—according to both Doe and Sue—"Gigi was more of a care-giver"; Doe "wasn't any good at that sort of thing." (Doe's brusque reaction when Sue called from the hospital with her diagnosis was typical not only of Doe's lack of care-giving skill, but of the kind of interaction mother and daughter had. Things did not improve as Sue's disease progressed.) Sue rejected any suggestion later that her decision to commit suicide was related to the experiences surrounding her own father's illness and death. She main-tained that her decision was independent, based solely on the death she faced if she endured to the end.

This complex family and social environment was to leave Sue a legacy of unresolved relational problems. It also endowed her with attitudes and skills that were rare, valuable but virtually unused in her daily life. Ironically, the disease that was killing her would also be the thing that created her. Amyotrophic lateral sclerosis would allow her to break through all her old barriers, fulfill her potential and become her authentic self. She would change from an ill, unknown, suburban housewife to a heroic, highly respected national figure and she would remain in that position, center stage, to the day she died. In the battle she was about to wage—a battle that many who held her beliefs had shunned—it didn't hurt at all that traces of the older generation's style marked her personality and permeated her manners. Nor that her expectations of everyone and everything were high, her relationships with others friendly but curtailed by subtle boundaries. In a time when mass media images create reality, Sue's aura of elegance added credibility to her cause.

September 1991

Following the first shock of learning that she had ALS, Sue became profoundly tense and depressed. She slept badly and became hypersensitive to the multiple signals of her weakening body. She realized that there had been perceptible signs for several months. The muscles in her hands and feet had shrunk. Her left arm was visibly thinner. Her jaw jerked occasionally, her calves were painful and all the massaging in the world didn't help.

The month passed in psychological pain and confusion. In late September, she drove to the rehabilitation section of the local hospital and saw there a world of oxygen masks, ventilators, hoists and pulleys, a world of total dependence on strangers, in which one cannot go to the toilet alone, scratch one's nose, bathe, eat. She was given pamphlets on palliative care, and these pamphlets described patients who were "surrounded by a loving family" or who found joy in "living a life of the mind." What loving family? she thought. What life of the mind? Let a genius like Stephen Hawking live a life of the mind. But me, if I cannot move my own body, I have no life. She wondered what she was doing there, felt she had no place in this corralled and crippled world.

Sue went home that night, stood before the mirror, looked at her athletic body, her thick titian-colored hair, her unlined face, her clear green eyes. She moved her limbs in slow, graceful motion, and tried to grasp that she would soon become what she had just seen. She had never doubted Dr. Eisen's final diagnosis. It answered everything. On another level it seemed insane.

She knew that she would never feel grateful merely to be alive, would never consent to sitting in a wheelchair passively waiting for death to arrive, cracking jokes, thinking positively. In the 12 years that she lived in California, from 1976 until she and Henry moved to Victoria in 1988, she had been a keen rock climber. Remembrances of those days now flooded her—the joy of reaching the top of the mountain, filling her lungs with cool air, breathing deeply, feeling close to the heavens and surveying the world spread out below. She'd loved the challenge, the stretching of herself, the triumph over odds. And she thought somewhere, someplace, there must be a cure.

The following day, Sue phoned Dr. Eisen and asked to participate in the experimental Lamotrigene program he had mentioned. This was a double blind study: half of the patients would receive Lamotrigene, half would receive a placebo, but neither the patients nor their doctors would be informed as to who received what. Soon after, Sue met with neurologist Donald Cameron at the ALS Clinic at Vancouver General Hospital. Dr. Cameron, a chemist as well as a physician, was pleased to have Sue in the program. The need for scientific studies into ALS, and on the effects of various drugs and treatments on the disease, was great. And there was an additional factor. About seven out of 100,000 persons develops ALS and the majority of those who contract the disease have well-defined, positive personalities. They are also intelligent, athletic, fit and non-smokers. Although she did not know it, Sue Rodriguez was a classic ALS victim.

While Sue struggled to cope with the realization that she had no future, that all her dreams were just illusions, her money worries and marital problems continued. She felt, too, that she'd been crazy to tell people she was terminally ill. She'd had little choice: all her friends had been waiting for the results of her diagnosis, and the moment she'd arrived home that day, the phone had started ringing. But the fact that it was terminal was more than some of her friends could take.

Said Sue: "Once they were aware that I was dying, they were either very uncomfortable knowing it or stricken with sorrow. And I found that it was tapping my energy. Each person I came across needed a different response. It wasn't like the birth of a child where everyone responds to the news in more or less the same way. With death you get all sorts of reactions. I found it draining, learning how each person was going to react and how to deal with it. I'd try to find the right words, to comfort them. You can't say 'Everything's going to be okay' when you know it's not. There were a number of friends who just couldn't face me. Or if they did, they'd talk around my diagnosis and pretend it wasn't happening. Slowly, most of them came around. Going public was the reason for that. It helped people talk about it openly."

One incident convinced Sue that she should have told no one. A week before Cole's school opened, Sue told the principal about her condition. The principal assured her it would be confidential. At the school to pick up Cole, she'd searched the billboard for the location of his classroom. Next to his name, for all the world to see, was a notation: "Mother ill."

Said Sue: "It enraged me so much that I went into the office and screamed and yelled at them, and told them how insensitive it was to do that, and I got one of the secretaries to wipe it out. They said it had been a terrible error but the damage was done. The whole school knew. I didn't want every kid or mother in the school sorry for Cole, or making remarks to him. When I got home, I called the vice-principal and really chewed him out. I was screaming at him so loud that my voice—I couldn't get over how high-pitched it was. It ended up being recorded on my tape machine. I remember playing it back a month later and I couldn't get over all the pain I was feeling. And I'd dumped it all on that poor man."

Henry's mother, who lives in Los Angeles, seemed simply unable to accept the fact that her daughter-in-law would die. Months passed before her mother-in-law could speak to Sue again. Sue felt her own mother and siblings were incapable of dealing with it. Doe disagrees: "We would have done anything in the world for her. She was quite secretive, told us very little. It almost seems from the moment she was born she didn't feel part of the family in the same way as the others. The illness only made it worse."

Sue and Henry were now in constant contact. She checked into her social security benefits, learned that both her Canada Pension and her U.S. Social Service benefits were available in advance to the terminally ill. These together totaled about $900 a month. But her deepest concern, and Henry's, was for their son. The city and province would provide all the home help services that she would need, but what of Cole? How could they best protect him? How could she teach him her values in the short time left? How could he be prepared for losing her? Wouldn't it be easier for Cole if his parents were both together? And wouldn't this make financial sense?

"Shortly before I was diagnosed, I'd been to Henry's apartment for dinner," Sue said. "We spoke of reconciliation. I couldn't even think about it. Even though I loved him, I knew there were problems that weren't going to be resolved, so I left him that night thinking, 'That's great, he really does love me, he's been through a mid-life crisis.' Then after I got my diagnosis, he came back. We should have taken time to think about the ramifications. We hadn't resolved any of our problems. We never had a chance with death looming over us. It was the worst decision."

Said Henry: "It was over long before her illness. I'd moved out and started another life. Sue had wonderful qualities and I wanted to help her, to be a good friend. You can't imagine how much I wanted that. And there were financial considerations. Sue wasn't going to be able to work again. I was trying to get my company going. I thought it would be better for Cole if I was in the house. I could also provide Sue with some physical security. But that wasn't what she wanted. She wanted me as a husband, totally and forever there. And I couldn't be that."

The realization that Henry had made a terrible mistake

in returning was to come only after weeks of intense but confused efforts to make the relationship work. In any case, it was never to be quite that simple. In the end, their presence became pure torment one to the other, yet their mutual animosity thrived alongside an equally powerful yearning to love and respect each other. This need to enhance each other's lives and not destroy them endured, and although it never worked, it's fair to say—if everything had to be balanced in the end—it prevailed.

These developments were to come only with time. In the early winter of 1991, Sue and Henry felt only one immediate need—to hold on to the house and provide Cole with a stable home and two parents. They took the house off the market and Henry moved back in. Deciding they might need some cash on hand in their unpredictable future, they took out a mortgage on the house. With their resources pooled, and a budget set up, they decided on a vacation. In October, they went to Hawaii.

Four

October 1991 to August 1992

Sue felt she had left behind a nightmare and reentered life once she reached the sun and sands of Hawaii. The illusion was short-lived. A few days later, she noticed a twitching in the muscle of her chest wall and a tickling in her throat whenever she ate. No matter what the food, or how much she chewed it, or how much water she swallowed, the tickling, the sense of tightness, would not go away. And then her voice, usually clear and sweet, took on a different tone, slightly hoarse and thick. On the flight back to Vancouver, she had difficulty breathing.

She checked with Dr. Cameron in the ALS Clinic at Vancouver General Hospital. It was clear to Cameron that Sue's condition had slightly but measurably deteriorated. Her body movements were stiffening, her muscle bulk decreasing and there were signs that the medulla oblongata, the lowermost portion of the vertebrate brain continuous with the spinal cord, was now involved. This controlled breathing, among other functions. Like Dr. Andrew Eisen, Donald Cameron had never been able to harden himself to the fate of ALS victims. He tried not to become emotionally involved but it was impossible. One patient after another over the years and he still found himself asking: How can she cope? What will happen to her family? What can I do to help? The answer to the last question was always the same: practically nothing. The only hope was in research. Somewhere in research lay the answer. If not a cure, at least a drug that would control the symptoms.

Sue had no such faith nor, she felt, the time. Her symptoms were progressing rapidly. In November, she told Dr. Cameron she was quitting the Lamotrigene program as it wasn't doing her any good. He felt there was no point in pressuring her, but as a scientist he was keenly disappointed. After all, it was simply a matter of taking the drug. Even though he didn't know if Sue was on Lamotrigene or the placebo, her staying on the program would at least have helped define its results.

Sue felt that traditional medicine was letting her down, and vowed to find a cure elsewhere. She tried acupuncture, going for several weeks to a clinic run by two Victoria physicians. They made no big promises, she said, but she gained the impression acupuncture might slow down the symptoms. No such thing happened. In any case, she couldn't keep up the visits. She was short of money; each visit cost $70, and initially she had to go two or three times a week.

Then Sue heard of Dr. Abe Hoffer, a Victoria psychiatrist who had done extensive work in vitamin therapy. She later described her visit: "I was shocked because I expected him to do an examination and be sort of optimistic on what he had to offer, but he was the opposite. His attitude was that he'd had a number of ALS patients and most of them hadn't responded to his therapy, although one person felt his muscles had improved. He told me to take COQ-10, something the Japanese have taken for many years. It's an expensive vitamin. I took it religiously for the prescribed time and it made no difference whatsoever. I was supposed to go back and report my findings. I didn't even bother."

The Christmas season came, and turned into a rare family gathering. Sue's youngest sister, Sally, and brother, Tom, came from Ontario, and on Christmas Day, Doe and her husband, Ken, and Sue's older sister, Barbara, with her common-law husband, Julian, came for dinner. In January, Barbara drove down again from her Vancouver Island farm to stay the weekend. They went into Victoria. Sue gave Barbara a list of things to do and buy for her while she went to the hairdresser. They lunched at a Mexican restaurant. "We had a good time, just sisters doing things together," said Barbara. "This was before Sue started to become really bitter toward our family. I could never understand why."

Meanwhile, Sue continued her search for a cure. She went to a masseuse whose technique was similar to rolfing. "She said her technique would cure just about everything," Sue recalled with a wry grin. "But it really wasn't any different from what I'd get from range-of-motion exercises. So I quit." Soon after, Sue read an article claiming that the mercury in dental fillings could poison the body. Sue had several amalgam fillings; the notion that she had simply been poisoned filled her with hope. Her condition was worsening, her feelings more despairing. In late February 1992, she and Henry went to a diagnostic center in Colorado Springs, Colorado, that specialized in alternative medicine. Sue had all her fillings removed and replaced. It cost $10,000 and did nothing to change her condition.

Sue's search for a miracle cure had followed a well-trodden path. Those who work with people suffering crippling or terminal illnesses see it all the time. In some cases, some alternate therapies give temporary relief. But others pretend to a cure, small matter that their success rate is unknown or nonexistent. They offer the illusion of hope, when the medical profession offers none. Traditional medicine dispenses medications that it trusts might help, offers the promise of making the dying patient comfortable and is honest about the ultimate reality—no cure and death assured. In these circumstances, the optimism furnished by alternative medicine wins out.

The trip to Colorado Springs was Sue's last bid for a miracle cure.

From the time of her diagnosis in August 1991, Sue had attended the monthly meetings of the ALS Society in Victoria. She was anxious to learn about the disease and to find out firsthand what drugs members had tried, what programs they'd been on, what worked and what didn't. When she attended a meeting in April 1992, following her return from Colorado Springs, her mood had changed. With all hope of a cure gone, she could see her own future in the faces and voices of the 25 other members whose scooters and hi-tech wheelchairs crowded the room.

That night she decided to commit suicide. Sue made this decision without fuss, hesitation or moral argument. The idea came and she accepted it. It felt right. The dominant nature of her disease was now clear. It would rob her of everything that gave value to her life and then slowly, at its own leisure, kill her. She did not fear pain: drugs could take care of that. She feared a drugged-out twilight of total dependency and hopelessness. Slowly, Sue was moving toward the position that she would steadfastly and publicly maintain for the next two years—that the quality of life is the essence of life, and that a life deprived of quality was not worth living.

Yes, she would commit suicide—but not yet. Despite everything, life was still good. Choosing the right time would be critical. She wanted to stay with Cole for as long as possible, but not leave him a memory of a mother paralyzed and drooling, unable to speak or hold her head up. If she stayed too long, that memory would haunt him into old age. She must spare him that and spare herself an undeserved and humiliating end. She dreaded above all else loss of control over her life. As long as she could speak, she could maintain it, but there would be no control over life or death once she lost her voice. That would be the time: when her voice started going, she would kill herself.

She did not tell Henry of her decision that night. She slept soundly and the next day drove into Victoria and bought a copy of *Final Exit*, the best-selling suicide manual by American Derek Humphry, founder of the Hemlock Society. For the next few days she thoughtfully perused it. The book spoke of suicide as "self-deliverance" and the phrase struck home. She was a proud and self-sufficient woman, one who'd always practiced responsibility for her own well-being. She would deliver herself from a death without dignity. Then the thought struck her that by the time her voice went, she would be incapable of lifting her hands to her mouth or swallowing a fatal overdose. To accomplish "self-deliverance" she'd need help.

Sue's life was now pointed in a direction that within months would thrust her into the national limelight. She had not been raised in any specific religious faith, and was generally unaware of the doctrinal investment that attached to questions of euthanasia and suicide. For a while when Sue was a child, Doe had been interested in the Baptist church and had taken all the children, but the experience had made little impression on Sue. She was oblivious to the fact that she was moving into an ethical and moral mine-field.

So Sue dropped by to talk to the family doctor, unaware of the momentous legal struggle that lay ahead, unaware that she was entering a battle that would continue long after her own life ended. What, she asked her doctor curiously, did he think about euthanasia? Taken aback, he brusquely said he'd never thought about it. A few days later, Sue went to another doctor. He was equally blunt, said he'd no wish to get mixed up in an illegal situation that could destroy him professionally.

These responses initially confused Sue. She had expected some sort of discussion, empathetic at least, if not supportive. They stuck in her mind and gradually she grew angry. There was nothing illegal in suicide; it wasn't a criminal act. The law allowed people to do it without condemning them. All she needed was someone to assist her to exercise a right that everyone else had. That is, everyone who wasn't physically disabled. The uneven nature of the law in practice—the able-bodied could commit suicide with impunity but those with a crippling disease couldn't—struck Sue as fundamentally unjust. It was her illness, her body, her death. She needed help—and she was determined to get it. But she didn't know where to turn. She didn't have forever. Week by week her body was changing. She walked now with a slightly rolling gait, all her graceful flexibility gone. When she swallowed food, she had to concentrate and make an effort.

In mid-May, Sue noticed in the local paper that a Toronto-based group called Dying With Dignity was meeting that week in the Victoria Public Library. She was thrilled. It sounded exactly like what she was looking for and she phoned Doe and asked her to come. She thought she would at last connect with like-minded people, people who didn't think it obligatory to hang on when everything that gave life value was gone. She was confident she'd get the information she needed to do what had to be done.

When they got to the meeting, the topic of discussion seemed to be the preparation of living wills, the circumstances that can surround the decision to accept or reject medical treatment, the clear allocation of decision-making authority before one faces a life-and-death crisis. None of this interested Sue. As far as she was concerned, rejecting medical treatment could simply result in a slow, inhuman death. She wanted a quick and dignified one. The non-criminalization of suicide in 1972 allowed her that. She whispered to Doe, and Doe stood up: "What do you think of someone's assisting a terminally ill relative to commit suicide?" she asked.

Dead silence. Some of the audience turned to stare at

Doe. Shy at the best of times, Doe was overwhelmed. She sat down, flustered and pink. Sue felt utterly let down. The meeting continued, the question unanswered.

A few days later, Sue phoned Clem Finney, the group's Victoria representative, and laid out her problem. He suggested she contact the Right To Die Society of Canada in Victoria. This society was set up to determine what rights people have under the charter to assistance in ending their lives. It received, on average, 10 to 15 requests per month for assistance in committing suicide.

Sue found she didn't have the energy to make the call. Her life was changing rapidly, all its familiar habits and comforts sliding away. She felt deeply depressed. Every week there were changes and adjustments that had to be made. Normally in spring she'd be outside with her wheelbarrow and gardening tools cleaning up the detritus of winter, hauling mulch and preparing the soil for the seedlings now springing up in their boxes. She'd zip down to the supermarket in Sidney, go for a walk, cook up a storm and she and Henry would have some friends in for dinner.

That life had gone, one piece at a time. Gardening, with its bending and stooping, was something she'd never do again. She'd loved power walking; that was finished too. She could still take short walks, but slowly, carefully, on the arms of a neighborhood friend such as Cathy Johnson. She'd fallen, a couple of times inside the house and a couple outside, going down like a puppet whose strings had snapped. She'd joked about being an old crock but the emotional pain had been worse that the physical pain. Her friends were hanging in there—friends such as Riki

Philpott, Liz Ferguson, Christine Tate, Cindy Ramsey, Catherine Gordon, Marg Owens—and during the first year of Sue's illness, Sue and Henry still gave the occasional dinner party, with Henry doing the cooking. Gradually, however, they stopped entertaining. While these friends did hang in to the end, because of Sue's weariness and the constant presence of busy professional workers, their visits became increasingly rare, to the point where, months before her death, they virtually ceased.

Sometimes she'd totally forget her condition. She'd be watching television and then remember something that had to be done. She'd start to leap up but her body would remain fixed on the couch. Or she'd want to brush her teeth and then find her fingers would no longer close on the handle, or do her hair and find her arm too stiff to lift. And to top it all off, Cole seemed upset that she'd no longer fool around with him. And Henry, more and more silent and edgy with the stress of trying to get a new business off the ground, had started coming home late for dinner a couple of nights a week.

Increasingly, Sue blamed her disease for the fact that Henry did not seem to love her. Her earlier understanding that he had returned for financial and supportive reasons had shifted. She now saw his return to the home after seven months of separation as essentially an attempt at reconciliation. Yet he had little to say to her and seemed to avoid her.

Later Sue would say: "I blame the ALS for the fact that the family structure isn't there anymore. It could have been ideal. Just before I was diagnosed, Henry and I were talking about getting back together again. So once I came home [after diagnosis] that's why it was so easy for us to decide to live together again, saying it was for Cole and financial reasons, to make it easier on all of us. But really it was a way of attempting to reconcile. But the disease didn't give us a chance. There were too many hurdles to jump over, it was too much of a challenge."

Said Henry: "Those times could have been so much better I wanted us to be at peace each other. I went back to be her friend, nothing else. I wanted to do everything I could for her and for our son. But our marriage was over. We'd lived apart for more than half a year. I couldn't pretend to a relationship that no longer existed. So I could do nothing to please her. I felt so guilty and she felt so rejected."

Early in August, six weeks after Clem Finney had suggested she call, and a year after her diagnosis, Sue phoned the Right To Die Society. A member, Anita Bundy, visited her, and soon after, Sue met the society's executive director, John Hofsess. The two hit it off at once. John was impressed by Sue's practicality, dignity and determination. Sue was impressed by John's kindness, straight talk and experience with questions of death and dying. Both had a strong sense of a meeting of minds.

Sue was by far the more powerful personality but both were equally self-directed. The friendship would last only six months. Hofsess, by his own actions, would be squeezed out of the picture and Sue would continue her fight without him. But those six months would be enough to activate a vehement national debate on the questions surrounding the continuation or the termination of life, and the linked concepts of human rights and death with dignity. The energy fueling this debate would not come solely from the age-old question of the moral appropriateness of terminating one's own life. It would also come from an awareness of society's increasing inability to control the forces of medical technology, and the difficulty institutions are experiencing in resolving the ethical issues resulting from this technology.

This debate would widen into a philosophical discussion of the question: to whom does life belong? It was a question that Sue herself would pose. It's fair to say that when Sue met John Hofsess, all the elements of her destiny fell into place.

Five

Sue Rodriguez was always clear about two things regarding her relationship with John Hofsess, who had founded the Right To Die Society of Canada a few months before they met: he did *not* counsel her to commit suicide—she'd determined on that course before they met; he *did* suggest she "break the silence" and go public with her bid for assisted suicide.

Hofsess was in his mid-fifties when he and Sue met, a mild-mannered, sad-looking man who had once been a successful journalist and was now utterly focused on death and dying. His professional life had had some curious highs and lows. For years he'd held the enviable position of film critic for *Maclean's* magazine. Then at one point, while living in New York and working for the now-defunct *Calgary Albertan*, he wrote a review of the horror movie *Friday the 13th* that was strikingly similar to one that had already been published in the *New York Times*. Hofsess said the word *plagiarism* was never used. He resigned of his own accord shortly after. He then wrote features for *Homemakers* and later became a copywriter—"a chocolate-chip hack," he called it—for the Loblaws trade newsletter, the *Insider's Report*.

In his years as a critic, Hofsess became friends with

Canadian film director Claude Jutra. When Jutra developed Alzheimer's disease in 1985, he asked Hofsess, who had written about euthanasia, for help in ending his life. Hofsess refused. Jutra's body was found on the shores of the St. Lawrence River in 1986. Hofsess couldn't forget Jutra's plea and his subsequent violent death: Jutra had apparently jumped from a bridge spanning the river. Three years later, Hofsess moved to Victoria to care for his ill 80-year-old mother, who died the following year.

In May 1991, cushioned by an $18,000 Canada Council grant given specifically for the project, Hofsess started working on a book that dealt with death and dying in Canada. Scarcely had he put pen to paper when Hofsess established the Right To Die Society of Canada, using the Canada Council grant to do so. This diversion of a literary grant into a personal pet project was not done in guilt-ridden secrecy. In the society's first newsletter, *Last Rights*, Hofsess, the self-appointed executive director, said he'd invested $19,500 of his own money in the society, much of it coming "from grants awarded by the Canada Council and the B.C. Ministry of Culture for development of my book."

The story came to light because Hofsess, short of funds, sought the remedy of a second $18,000 Canada Council grant. When it was refused, he naively asked the council whether "politics" had played a role. Given this combination of dubious initiative, idealism and credulity, the friendship between John Hofsess and a self-directed woman like Sue Rodriguez was destined for a short run and an abrupt end. Yet it was Hofsess's skill in orchestrating media coverage on a subject generally considered so distasteful as to be taboo that set the entire direction of Sue's future.

When Sue met with John Hofsess, she was totally frustrated, not knowing where to turn for help in arranging her own demise at a time of her own choosing. Hofsess, with his media background, likely saw this calm, attractive woman as a potential star, the perfect vehicle for the long-awaited opportunity to promulgate his own beliefs. These, in essence, were that compassion for a suffering human being was the highest good, and in an enlightened society, the giving of a merciful death for those who seek it is an act of love above and outside the proper realm of criminal law.

Hofsess told Sue she had two options. The first was to commit suicide privately. Someone would be found to help her. He'd do it himself, if need be. To prove his sincerity, Hofsess drew up a contract guaranteeing that he would assist Sue in "terminating her life at a time of her own choosing, preferably by permission of Canadian law but failing that, by the moral authority of personal conscience."

(Henry watched this relationship with some amazement: "Here was this person, inside my own home, offering to kill my wife, even drawing up a contract to do it—and he'd only just met her.")

The second option, Hofsess said, was to ask for a court ruling as to whether a disabled person has a right to assisted suicide. This legal action, he said, would "break the silence" on the virtually taboo subject of physician-assisted suicide.

It is difficult to say with certainty what Sue's motivations were when she decided to go public. She would be asked that question many times in her two remaining years. Why didn't she commit suicide quietly and privately, with anonymous help, as others do? A censorious undertone usually ran through this query, as if Sue had acted in dubious taste, had even been a little self-aggrandizing in attempting to redress her plight in a public manner. These misgivings were without grounds. By nature Sue was a very private person, and totally devoid of any vulgar yearning for the limelight. Later she came to enjoy it, but she never had any need for it, and it played no part in her original decision.

So why did she spend the last months of her life making such an issue of her situation? At various times, Sue herself would give various answers. None was inconsistent with any other, and as her involvement in the case progressed, it is likely that Sue refined what were originally intuitive, sometimes inarticulate, reasons.

When Hofsess proposed that she go to court, and Sue agreed, undoubtedly the prime issue for her was self-determination. Sue was a woman of strong convictions and a powerful sense of self. She had control over her life and preferred to have control over her death. She had become aware of the ways in which ALS victims die and wanted none of it. She was legally entitled to commit suicide and saw the deprivation of this right, by nature of her illness, as an inequitable situation that the court could redress.

Sue knew that other people, dying of terminal illnesses, were in an identical situation. Her belief in self-determination extended to others. She was going to die anyway. Why not fight for her beliefs? Maybe it would also help others. She saw herself as an up-front person, not one to go behind the law. Said Sue: "I have a son. I want him to respect the law. I don't want my last act on earth to be tainted by illegality. But if I can't obey the law in the end, I'll know at least I did all I could to change it. So will he."

So Sue agreed to go public. She and Hofsess approached Chris Considine, a 39-year-old trial lawyer who had been on a treadmill of controversial, high-profile cases for the past five years. Considine had been consistently astute in identifying precedent-setting cases and he found this one irresistible. It would be the first time Canada had dealt with the issue of doctor-assisted suicide, a move Considine saw as long overdue.

Considine's opening salvo to the attorney general of British Columbia was a request for the court to assure that a physician who helped Sue Rodriguez to die would not be prosecuted. This request was, in effect, a warning shot and really a media tease, for no such assurance could possibly be given, even off the record. Such an assurance would be in direct contradiction to Section 241(b) of the Criminal Code, which states that anyone who counsels or aids a person to commit suicide is liable to a maximum of 14 years' imprisonment. However, the media picked up the thorny issue and it moved into the public arena.

While this was going on, Hofsess had devised a brilliant plan to ensure that the principles he so intensely believed in gained national attention. A parliamentary committee in Ottawa was studying the "recodifying" of both the general and specific parts of the 100-year-old

Criminal Code. This included sections that dealt with euthanasia. Hofsess arranged for a videotaped statement made by Sue to be played before this committee. This five-minute tape was eloquent, passionate and moving. He then notified the media of the coming event. Before the standing committee on justice and the then-Justice Minister Kim Campbell had heard a word of it, Sue's eloquent plea had resounded across the country. The legal issues on which Considine would base his court strategy were evident in the rhetoric, which said in part:

"The deterioration which I am undergoing is acceptable to me, up to a point. Beyond that point, my life will have degenerated to mere biological existence. I will become a helpless victim of my illness and have to endure prolonged suffering, lasting many months or even years.

"This is not acceptable to me. But when I sought legal advice as to my options, I was told that it is legal for someone to commit suicide in Canada—but it is not legal for someone like myself, who lacks the motor skills to terminate my own life, to ask for or receive any assistance in ending my life.

"Why it should be illegal for someone to assist me to do something that is legal is a paradox I will never understand. But more to the point, it is a paradox that forces me to suffer greatly—both mentally and physically.

"If my suffering was being inflicted upon me in any other context, it would be called an abuse of human rights at the very least, and might well be called a crime. But because it happens in the name of modern medicine, I am supposed to accept whatever indignities my illness inflicts upon me and keep quiet.

"If my doctors relieve my suffering, I am not supposed to say anything. And if politicians won't change the law, I'm supposed to be helpless and powerless and not make my suffering known—to die in quiet desperation, the way that most terminally ill people do.

"I want to ask you, gentlemen, if I cannot give consent to my own death, then whose body is this? Who owns my life?"

"Who owns my life?" The words rang out like a battle cry. Opponents of all types of euthanasia heard in it the potential of a major assault on both their beliefs and their entrenched legal and political positions. National groups representing the handicapped and disabled also identified the case as critical, but their interests were more complex, their stance less cut-and-dried. They were sensitive to the vulnerability of the disabled and the tendency of society to devalue their lives—and they were equally concerned that the competently made wishes of the handicapped be respected. Their stake was not only in the final outcome of the case, but also in the direction in which it proceeded.

In the meantime, B.C. attorney general Colin Gablemann had told Considine that he would not offer legal protection to anyone who helped Sue Rodriguez die. Police would decide whether the Criminal Code had been violated. Considine promptly filed an application in the Supreme Court of British Columbia asking for "a declaration that the operation of Section 241 of the Criminal Code violates Sue Rodriguez's constitutionally guaranteed rights and that neither Sue nor any physician assisting her to attempt to commit or to commit suicide, will by that means commit any offense against the law."

The ultimate goal for this application was to allow Sue to die with dignity at the time and by the means she herself chose. The order Considine sought would clear the way for a physician to set up an intravenous line containing a fatal drug which Sue would be able to start flowing into her body by flicking a switch. To get this order, Considine would have to challenge the Criminal Code provisions that made assisted suicide illegal.

In law the Charter of Rights and Freedoms dominates. If the court finds any legislation that violates it, that legislation is null and void. Considine challenged the assisted-suicide provision under three separate sections of the charter, Sections 7, 12 and 15 (1). Section 7 deals with the right to life, liberty and security of the person; Section 12 with the right not to be subjected to cruel and unusual treatment or punishment; and Section 15 (1) deals with the equality of every individual before the law without discrimination based on race, ethnic origin, color, religion, sex, age or mental or physical disability.

December 17, 1992 was set as the date to hear the petition in the Supreme Court of British Columbia.

As these legal lines were drawn, Sue's life was being transformed. Sue had always felt good about herself. She was essentially a happy self-starter, with a clear idea of what she wanted and a strong sense of her own dignity and value. Some members of her own family even thought her a bit of a snob, a fact which Sue found funny. "Must be because my nose turns up, " she laughed. But her self-esteem had taken a terrible battering in the months previous to meeting John Hofsess. She'd gone downhill rapidly, but worse yet was a horrid sense that she was becoming irrelevant to everyone. She was struggling to accept Henry simply as a friend—and until the day she died she sincerely described Henry as "the best friend I ever had"—but she wanted Henry to be hers. Finding herself facing death, she needed that comfort, that assurance. But Henry had his own integrity: he couldn't be something he wasn't. The pain of that was unbearable. At 42, Sue felt as though she were 82, tossed out of the mainstream, put on the rubbish heap and rendered voiceless. The shock of knowing she was dying had been terrible, but the realization that she would lose control of everything long, long before the end was almost as bad. And when she had spoken of this to her doctors, and tried to change it by arranging her own death, she'd been brushed off as if her suggestions were criminal.

But as Hofsess orchestrated his publicity and Considine made his legal moves, Sue began to see direction in her future and perhaps meaning to her fate. Nothing would change the descending spiral of her remaining months, but they might not be, after all, a time of meaningless desperation.

Sue's sense of healthy self-esteem was slowly restored as the media sought to interview her. Within a month of her meeting with Hofsess, a highly readable piece written by him—"Will Sue Rodriguez Go Gently Into That Good Night?"—was published in the *Globe and Mail*. This was the second national exposure of Sue's story (the CBC's "Journal" had run a feature), and the title brilliantly reflected the inherent power of the subject. Death remains the one consummate certainty in these uncertain times. The "good night" awaits everyone, the ultimate adjudicator of equal rights. For most people this reality is bad enough, but between life and the "good night" there now exists godlike medical technology capable of indefinitely prolonging the whole business of relinquishing life and entering death. The thought of falling victim to its potions and apparatus, with their ability not so much to sustain life as give an obscene imitation of it, is more frightening to most people than death itself. This increasing fear of being plugged in, pumped up, and recycled—as much as the pathos of Sue's plight and the boldness of her legal fight—made the Rodriguez story one of enormous consequence.

In early November, *Maclean's* ran a full page on the issue, including a warm, laughing picture of Sue with Hofsess, under its law section. Then the CBC invited Sue and Hofsess to appear as guests on its vintage program "Front Page Challenge." Sue was thrilled. Sharon Bartlett, an independent film producer who lives in Vancouver, and who created the documentary *Who Owns My Life*, a biography of Sue, remembers that night:

"I'd contracted to produce a film for the CBC on Sue and had started to work on it. So I went to the CBC studios to watch them film the show. The usual panel was there— Pierre Berton, Allan Fotheringham, Jack Webster, Betty Kennedy. Debbie Wilson of the *Globe and Mail* was also there. She'd interviewed Sue. Sue didn't get a chance to be herself. She was asked only one or two questions. Fotheringham spent most of the time needling John.

"We'd arranged that afterward John, Sue and I would have dinner with Svend Robinson. Svend was then political consultant of the Right To Die Society and he and Sue were anxious to meet each other. Sue was staying at the Four Seasons, so after the show we went back there and had dinner in Le Pavilion.

"Sue looked wonderful and was in high spirits. She had a terrific sense of humor and we spent a lot of the evening laughing. From the moment they met, Sue and Svend got on well together. When you do that kind of story, standard rules of journalism don't hold. You can't be as removed as you'd normally be. Sue and I became friends, not best friends, but really good friends. She had such a clarity of mind, a fantastic sense of humor, but above all she had the wonderful gift of knowing precisely what was right for her.

"I wanted to film them all together—John, Svend and Sue—but the hotel manager wouldn't allow my camera crew into the dining room. He said there might be a couple dining together who shouldn't be and the camera might catch them. We laughed about that but in fact we lost some really good film . . . their first meeting . . . when you remember their last."

In late November, Sue's videotaped appeal was played before the Ottawa parliamentary committee studying the Criminal Code. Sue's plea was immediately opposed in a brief presented by two pro-life activists, Cheryl Eckstein of the Surrey, B.C.-based Compassionate Healthcare Network, and Toronto-based Campaign Life Coalition director, Sabina McLuhan. Eckstein and McLuhan grossly distorted the issue by arguing that there was a connection between the legal exemption Rodriguez sought for herself and Nazi death camps. Whatever validity their stand against euthanasia might have, it was totally undermined when McLuhan played a tape of a Nazi propaganda film that justified euthanasia, and pointed out that this mindset had resulted in mass, government-sanctioned killings. At the committee's conclusion, Section 241(b) remained intact.

Meanwhile, back in B.C. in mid-November, two groups that recognized a serious threat to current legislation outlawing euthanasia decided to apply for intervenor status in the forthcoming Supreme Court of British Columbia hearing. On behalf of the Pro Life Society of British Columbia, which joined the Pacific Physicians for Life Society, Hilda Kreig contacted lawyer Ace Henderson of Davis & Company, a prestigious law firm established in Vancouver in 1892. Henderson is a genial, fiftyish Q.C., very much at ease with himself, the world and his highly successful slot in it.

He remembers the interview with Kreig, who is president of the Pro Life Society, because she asked him what his personal views and beliefs were. Most clients don't do that and he explained that it was irrelevant. As this reply seemed unsatisfactory, he allowed that he had a vague sympathy for their position and was not fervently committed to their cause. Kreig left. Henderson thought he would never see her again. However, she came back and he agreed to take the case. He immediately submitted an affidavit applying for intervenor status. This is not automatically granted: there has to be a good reason that someone should be allowed to run interference in someone else's affairs. The judge granted it immediately.

On Cromarty Avenue in Saanich, Sue was surprised at the number of supportive cards and letters she was receiving, and she gratefully acknowledged these with a note. Of course, there were also disapproving letters, but with rare exception Sue made no attempt to respond to them. She was not a woman who felt obligated to acknowledge others' beliefs; in fact, she seemed utterly indifferent to them. It is interesting to note, though, that later, when she met Victoria businesswoman Helma Libick, who was to become a great friend, Sue asked her to make two files of the correspondence: the supportive letters—a thick file—were placed in the top drawer of the cabinet; the rest—some hoping she would accept fate and trust in God, several letters from academics and physicians laying out reasons that changes to the anti-euthanasia laws were undesirable, some wild herbal "cures" and vitamin "cures"—were filed in the bottom of the cabinet at the back. It was almost as if she thought proximity of criticism might contaminate the power of the approving letters.

Said Sue in summing up these months: "What I liked about rock climbing was getting to the top. I was frightened to death, really scared, but when you finally made it the feeling was indescribable. All the support I started to get stirred up that old feeling. Suddenly I thought, 'Hey! Maybe I've still got a climb to do, a mountaintop to reach!' The thought I still could accomplish something was wonderful."

By the time the case opened before Mr. Justice Allen Melvin in Victoria on December 17, 1992, Sue Rodriguez was fast becoming a national figure. She slid into the role as if her entire life had been a preparation for it, which indeed it had.

Six

Law courts can be places of exquisite boredom and death-less torpor. The very issue of some cases, however, is the stuff of high drama, and in those trials or hearings the court unwittingly becomes a theater, a stage upon which the feelings unleashed by the issue are contained only by the well-established protocol of manners and procedures. The architecture, the furnishings, the black gowns—everything is designed to elicit earnestness, to ensure that all persons present understand that justice is the foundation of society and law the cement. In a society where barely anyone stands for anyone else, the courtroom leaps to its feet as one when the judge enters, and remains standing until His Lordship sits. A sheriff stands here, another one there. The lawyers, intervenors or prosecutors, are all in place brimming with quiet cordiality one to the other while planning one another's humiliating defeat. The public is discouraged from talking. Whispering is the order of the day. A coughing fit can mean expulsion.

Such was the mood in the Victoria courtroom on December 17, 1992, when Sue Rodriguez arrived to plead her cause. Her husband was by her side, along with John Hofsess, and member of Parliament Svend Robinson, who only eight days earlier had introduced a private member's bill designed to amend the Criminal Code to allow for physician-assisted suicide at a patient's request. (The bill is currently being redrafted.)

The emotion didn't arise from the sight of Sue's bright smile or wasted frame as Svend pushed her wheelchair past a score of reporters and cameramen, or later from the sound of her calm voice, weakened and flattened by illness, as she carefully addressed the bench. It was the issue itself: it turned all normal values upside down. There she sat, serenely asking Mr. Justice Allen Melvin to interpret the law so that she could put enough poison into her body to close down her lungs and stop her strong, proud heart from beating.

Small wonder that Judge Melvin listened with a face of stone. He'd been chief prosecutor for the city of Vancouver for years before appointment to the bench in 1990. A tough law-and-order advocate, he'd worked his way through scores of tangled issues where law and justice had grappled with each other for dominance. He hadn't hesitated to allow the Pro Life Society of British Columbia and the Pacific Physicians for Life Society to intervene. The views of others demanded to be heard in a case as significant as this.

Chris Considine laid out his arguments with the precision of a microsurgeon. The core of his case was to show that the Criminal Code law making it illegal to counsel, aid or abet suicide was contrary to the Charter of Rights and Freedoms. With respect to Section 7 of the charter, he argued that the application was *not* based upon a right to die, but rather on three points: the right for Sue to live her remaining life with the inherent dignity of a human being; the right to control what happens to her body while she is living; and the right to be free from governmental interference in making fundamental personal decisions concerning the terminal stages of her life.

Considine drew many parallels to the former abortion law, which was struck down because it was found to contravene "security of person" by preventing a woman from having autonomy over her body.

Next, in the respectful but slightly chippy tone of a barrister who relishes dissent, he turned to Section 12. It was, he claimed, cruel and unusual treatment to force Sue to continue to exist and undergo medical procedures to keep her alive, all dignity gone, and her life prolonged by only a few weeks. Finally, he focused on Section 15 (1) of the charter, charging that the Criminal Code section had the effect of discriminating against Sue because it allowed able-bodied persons to commit suicide while making it illegal for those whose incapacity required they seek assistance in ending their lives.

He concluded his constitutional arguments with a dash of rhetoric: "What a paradox when a patient can legally disconnect a life support system and die, but that Ms Rodriguez cannot arrange for a doctor-assisted suicide!"

He then read three affidavits into evidence. The first statement was from Sue's current family doctor, Donald Lovely. (This affidavit was later quoted at length in the dissenting opinion of the Honourable Chief Justice Allan McEachern when the case went on to the B. C. Court of Appeal.)

Dr. Lovely described in detail the different initial signs of ALS, adding that the wretched latter stages are roughly similar in all victims. He spoke of muscle wasting throughout the entire body, including the muscles of the head, neck and throat, all of which makes it hard, and eventually impossible, to speak, chew or swallow. The muscles used in breathing also become weak, and as it becomes impossible to cough and clear secretions, respiratory infections and choking on food or secretions are a danger.

Said Dr. Lovely: "Terminally they are likely to be completely paralyzed in all of their limbs, and unable to support even the weight of their head. They must be suctioned for secretions. They are dependent [on being turned] to prevent pressure sores . . . and require help for urinary and bowel care. If a patient chooses they may elect to have a feeding tube placed through their abdominal wall into their stomach if they can no longer chew or swallow. Patients may also elect to have a tracheotomy tube placed in their neck into the airway so they can have assisted breathing either through administration of oxygen or in some cases with respirators. Throughout all this a person's intellectual functions aren't affected so there's total awareness of what is going on.

"I believe that death usually results because of the weakness in the muscles of breathing and swallowing. The patients may aspirate and choke to death on food; aspiration of food or secretions may lead to pneumonia; or the muscles used in breathing may simply become so weak that they cannot breathe well enough to maintain life. [Some] help exists to cope with the disease symptoms but these become less satisfactory as the illness progresses, so that I believe this does become a very hard disease to suffer.

"The patient has not only the emotional anguish of knowing they have an invariably fatal illness, but also must suffer more and more in an immediately physical sense. Terminally, the patient is totally dependent [on others] for the most basic requirements of daily life."

Considine then read into the record a report from Sue's neurologist, Dr. Donald Cameron. Dr. Cameron's report noted that the usual cause of death is a "respiratory insufficiency because of marked weakness of respiratory muscles," a nice way of saying Sue would be asphyxiated. There were no medications to slow the symptoms nor would there likely be for some time.

Dr. Cameron said he'd reexamined Sue a month earlier, and assessed her life expectancy to be between six and 18 months. "Regarding further progression, I anticipate Ms Rodriguez will lose her voice and be completely unable to speak [or] swallow food orally within the next few weeks to months. I also anticipate that she will be bedridden and/or in a wheelchair permanently within the next few weeks and with progressive respiratory muscle involvement she will become short of breath at rest, in bed, or in a wheelchair."

When Dr. Sandra Elder was called upon to speak, she emphasized for the record that Sue was not trying to make any decisions for anyone else, that the ruling would apply to her alone.

Then it was Sue's turn. She had been helped out of her wheelchair and sat, not in the witness box, but in the counsel area. All eyes were riveted on her ramrod-straight-backed figure, her copper-colored head, the long tapering fingers on permanently crumpled hands. Leaning forward, everyone in the courtroom strained to catch each slow and carefully enunciated word. Every sentence or two Sue would pause and, with difficulty, swallow.

"I want to be in charge of my life and my death," she declared. Her voice was thin and without any change in tone or pitch. "I just feel an inner guidance tells me that it's the right thing for me to do and I should be allowed to do it. I would like that option because I feel that I don't want to die a gruesome death of trying to get air or to go into a choking spasm or starve. My muscles are slowly atrophying and the airway will close down. My muscles will be unable to push food down my throat. I will die of choking, asphyxiation or pneumonia."

Sue later described her testimony as "essentially a plea for help." She said she loathed describing the manner of her possible demise, which is easy to imagine as normally Sue dreaded saying anything to anyone, even Henry, that could be interpreted as seeking sympathy or showing self-pity. She simply wanted the facts out. She believed that anyone hearing the realities of the fate awaiting her could not condemn her to it. Her own tendency would probably have been to go away, to have died quietly, she said. But Hofsess had "planted the seed to go public and it grew." She felt appreciative toward Hofsess for this until the day she died.

Now, making her statement, she paused for breath. Looking full-faced at Mr. Justice Melvin, Sue said: "I feel that it is my right to die with dignity. I do not want to die of pneumonia or choking, and I do not want my family to endure the stress of watching me slowly deteriorate and die. I do not want palliative care, which would involve injections of morphine to relieve the pain. I choose to be alert and aware of my surroundings before I go."

Life was still good, she said. She enjoyed each day and experienced happiness with her family. "I want to be able to live as long as possible and to have the option [of suicide] at a time I feel I do not want to experience any more discomfort. I feel it's a choice I should make for myself."

Sue had laid out the facts as if she were speaking of the weather. A long silence followed her conclusion. The empathy for her was palpable. Innocent of any crime or wrongdoing, she appeared trapped, a prisoner on death row awaiting execution by the state. There's wasn't a person in the courtroom who would have let an animal suffer the slow death her doctors had described. But Sue was a human being and, as lawyer Johannes Van Iperen of the federal justice department was about to point out, subject to laws that had been drawn up for the larger good of society.

The Criminal Code did not conflict with the provisions of the charter, Van Iperen asserted. The right to life, liberty and security—which is viewed as guaranteeing freedom of choice—does not include the right to commit suicide or to assist suicide. When Parliament decriminalized suicide in 1972, he pointed out, it certainly wasn't with the intention of encouraging suicide, nor was it to protect a right to die. Suicide was decriminalized largely because its criminality was redundant: who was there to punish for doing it?

"The waiver of the right to life does not become a constitutionally protected right to die," he told the bench. This had Mr. Justice Melvin wondering aloud whether the right to liberty and freedom of choice would not involve the right to choose one's own death. Van Iperen assured His Lordship that it did not, that freedom of choice involves only the liberty to do something positive. Many choices are not constitutionally protected.

Van Iperen also pointed out that while charter provisions dealing with cruel and unusual treatment might apply to Sue Rodriguez, they would not apply to the person assisting her to die.

At this point, Mr. Justice Melvin adjourned the hearings until the following morning.

Sue had been well aware that the justice department would intervene to protect its own laws, so she was prepared for opposition from that quarter. She seemed to be quite unprepared for the assault on her case launched the following day by Ace Henderson, representing the Pacific Physicians for Life Society and the Pro Life Society of British Columbia.

Since going public three months earlier, Sue had become something of a star, a nationally recognized personality. Only three people had publicly criticized or questioned her suicide efforts—Cheryl Eckstein, Sabina McLuhan and Marilyn Seguin of Dying With Dignity. Seguin's criticism had been muted, ambivalent. After appearing before the same parliamentary sub-committee as Eckstein and McLuhan, she had said her heart was with Rodriguez, but not her head. She had said it wasn't unusual for the terminally ill in Canada to commit suicide secretly with a doctor's help and she believed that making euthanasia legal would in fact make it more difficult to obtain. The briefs of these three intervenors had been presented in Ottawa, at a distance, as it were, from Sue, and the publicity they received had been slight compared to the space given Sue's dramatic videotaped message.

There's a danger that attaches to playing a heroic role in public life: the hero tends to integrate the image that has been created in playing the role. Criticism then becomes that much harder to cope with. Sue now reacted this way in the face of Ace Henderson's intervention. After months of almost undiluted praise, interviews, television appearances, she now confronted opponents who did not in the least approve of her or the way she was behaving, and, in fact, considered her a threat to the aged and handicapped.

She was a newcomer to the psychological carnage that can take place in the courtroom. Before her diagnosis, she had not had reason to ponder the larger issues, such as the tensions that exist between the good of the individual and the good of society. Law to her was the embodiment of justice, which, of necessity, must include compassion. She was unaware that laws are words often clumsily hammered together in an attempt to impose constructs that will benefit society at large, and that the good of the individual is often subsumed in their interpretation.

Sue herself was not subject to personal criticism or cross-examination. Only a lawyer with a death wish would have put her on the stand. In any case, she could have handled that. What she found deeply painful was the face-on meeting with others who were determined to stop her from getting the help she needed. They were not faced with the prospect of a hideous death. She was not asking them to commit suicide, was not imposing her beliefs on them. They could die as they wished. What sort of people would want to impose their beliefs on her and everyone else? Why was there no respect for her hard-won values, her conscience? Sue was often to reveal an extraordinary naïveté as to how society worked. She viewed these interventions not as a legitimate part of a national dialogue on a critical issue, but almost as meddling in her personal life.

She listened intently as Henderson sought an order that the appeal be dismissed. He described the Pro Life Society of British Columbia, and Pacific Physicians for Life Society—an organization of 250 practicing physicians—as "devoted to the sanctity of human life." He noted that one is not legally required to extend one's life by artificial means such as a life-support system. But that is quite different from directly and intentionally acting to end one's life.

Henderson hammered on the point that life is sacred: "The law against assisted suicide exists because Parliament believes that some fundamental values, in this case the sanctity of life, are of sufficient importance to justify intrusions on personal autonomy," Henderson told the bench. "Unless Ms Rodriguez can show that she has a right or freedom to commit suicide under Section 7, she lacks any charter-based claim. There has never been a right to commit suicide. In fact, until 21 years ago, it was a crime."

He went on to say that whether one is terminally ill or

not is beside the point. If the right to be free from state interference in matters of bodily integrity, or psychological stress, existed, then all competent adults would have "a right to suicide." But no such right exists in law.

"And if it did," said Henderson, "it wouldn't be restricted to the terminally ill. Furthermore, doctors would not be the only ones exempt from punishment or sanctions in assisting suicide, as it does not require the skill of a physician to kill another person."

Henderson was painting a picture of a society where suicide would not merely be passively decriminalized (as it is today) but would be viewed as an active right, to be exercised like any other right. Not only would people commit suicide at will, but anyone could help them do it with impunity. Having conjured up a nightmare of a society in which murder could easily pass as suicide— particularly in the deaths of the aged or disabled— Henderson spoke again about the sanctity of life, the need to preserve and value it and the irreconcilable conflict of duties into which physicians would be drawn if legislation allowed patients to demand help from them to commit suicide.

Henderson said that if the public wanted change in the euthanasia law, then Parliament was the place where this should be negotiated. But the courts were not the place. He concluded by reading affidavits from other ALS victims, their families or friends who opposed Sue's application because medical care and love could procure "a peaceful outcome."

At this point, tears that had been pooling fell from Sue's eyes. She could not raise her hand to wipe them away from her cheeks. They sat there and dried. She was exhausted from two days of hearings, wounded by the evidence of lack of compassion and stunned that fellow ALS sufferers would not at least have stayed neutral.

She felt at that moment a crushing despair at people's inability to respect the truths of others, at their unwillingness to understand the uniqueness of each human life. More than anything, she felt that those who were healthy and in the midst of life really did not care about the sufferings of the dying. They chose not to enter that world with open hearts to see the realities, to realize that the rules that work for the able and living become, like almost everything else, irrelevant to the needs of the dying.

Outside the courtroom, she simply said: "Those people are not me."

Seven

Christmas 1992

Christmas came as Sue sat at home waiting for the judgment of Mr. Justice Melvin. Like most ritualistic family events, Christmas was a time of mixed elation and tension. Sue know this might be her last Christmas with Cole and she was resolved that he remember it as a loving family event.

This need of Sue's to create a family for her son, a family with its own traditions, endured to the end, even in the face of multiple bitter and discouraging realities. She knew from her own childhood that a rich mulch of memories can be the most important legacy—for good or for bad—that a parent can leave a child. She was desperate to build a bank of them for Cole in the time that remained to her. She knew, because he was only eight, that most of his life's memories would come into existence after she'd gone—and almost certainly after she'd been replaced by another woman, young, healthy and probably beautiful. She felt pain but no resentment: she longed only to secure a small place for herself among her son's memories.

Sue organized a Christmas dinner and drew up a list of gifts, which Henry willingly shopped for. Doe, Barb and Julian came again for a turkey dinner. Henry was loving and attentive. But despite their mutual efforts, the dinner, served in midafternoon, was strained. Doe and Julian smoked, but because Sue was susceptible to breathing difficulties, and because she disliked the habit, they had to do their smoking outside in the cold. They had driven down, fancied a few stiff drinks, but hesitated to take more than a couple of glasses because of the long drive home. Everyone did their best to be jolly but there was little spontaneous joy. The guests left early.

Sue was once again reminded of the discrepancy that existed between the image she projected in the media and the realities at home. Her public image was that of a good-looking, determined woman with a handsome, professional husband, an excellent address and prestigious legal and political support for her cause. This picture was partly true. At the same time it was essentially false: it projected a powerful assumption that this woman's private life would be rich in love and support.

In fact, Sue's network of support, outside of professional help, was fragile and extremely limited. While she was being looked after by a virtual army of home-makers and health-care workers coming and going ten hours a day, they were hired professionals. Sue had moved a lot in her life, and although she had many friends in many places, she had very few longtime friends and none around her now.

She and Henry had moved to Victoria only three years before her diagnosis. Her friends were neighbors, or people she had met while working or attending the Divorce Lifeline group. Her relationships with them were warm but comparatively new. There was not a shared history of triumphs and failures, old incidents and common acquaintances that, in time of crisis, creates among friends a unique source of comfort and support. Her friends were sterling and did what they could; however, for safety's sake, she now required trained help to do almost anything. She could barely walk 20 feet now, even with support. By the end of each day, her entire upper body would suffer from spasms, a sudden tightening of the remaining muscle that, while not painful, left her totally locked, immobile and frightened.

Except for Henry, no family member looked after her. Doe said she would do anything in the world for Sue, but putting her intentions into practice called for strengths she could not find.

"When Sue first became ill," Doe said, "I wanted to be with her, to be there for her. Then someone came in to give her a bath, then massages, and then she started giving interviews. I felt I wasn't included in these things, and felt I was neither wanted nor necessary. There were two horrible days when her care-givers couldn't come and I went down to fill in. I was terrified. Anyway, these days to go down just for an hour's visit—it's a long way."

Doe's feelings of helplessness and her inability to cope, coupled with her sense that Sue had all the help she needed, left them both free of the hard and painful work required to build a strong bond between them. Sue's sister, Barb, guilelessly reinforced Doe's feelings, for she too felt that Sue did not really want them around. Barb had always been aware of Sue's "difference" and the fact that Sue had been her grandparents' favorite. A statement from Doe shows that Sue as a young child had already started to differentiate herself from her immediate family: "Sue wasn't close to me, as the other girls were." Unwillingly, they were caught in a web of relationships woven over 30 years ago in Ontario, a web whose meaning had long since dissipated, but whose power to trap its victims into a fixed position still held.

Doe is a tenderhearted sensitive being. As a young woman she had been totally unprepared to deal head-on with the powerful family into which she'd married. Like all well-raised young ladies of her day, she had been taught not to express what she felt. Her anger at Sue for adoring a grandmother who had raped her daughter-in-law's ego, disempowered her and turned her into a silent, suffering victim, had long been driven underground. Doe's wounds from those years had never healed, and central to them was Sue's choice of the stylish, manipulative, self-willed Gigi as her mentor.

Doe was sincere when she described herself as not being a care-giver. She was incapable of a care-giving, maternal relationship with her dying daughter because there had rarely been any truth, understanding or forgiveness between them. This did not mean that she did not love her daughter and anguish over her fate. "I am sure," said Sue's brother, Tom, "that my mother cried herself to sleep many a night. But as a family, we don't express ourselves that much."

For a while, when Sue lived in California, she and Doe developed a fond and spontaneous relationship. But it did not survive time and changed circumstance. Sue moved to Victoria; Doe was widowed for the second time; Sue became ill, and the closeness evaporated.

Now surrounded by busy, professional help, Sue, no doubt unconsciously, reinforced Doe's feelings of help-lessness. But this reinforcement was perhaps not entirely innocent. Children admire and respect strong parents. Although Sue had adored her grandmother, she had as a child felt keenly the secondary place her parents held in relationship to Gigi and H.V. A strong and willful child herself, she watched with disdain her mother's passivity, Doe's inability to put her parents-in-law in their place. Traces of that old resentment, of the child's disrespect for the loser, still coursed through Sue's feelings toward her mother. When Doe said, "There was nothing I could do for Sue," hers was not the voice of callousness or indiffer-ence. It was the voice of a woman speaking a truth about herself, a woman who had been unable to stand up for her own life. It was also the voice of a woman undergoing a major personal tragedy of her own—entirely apart from the fact that her daughter was dying. In March 1992, Ken Thatcher, Doe's husband of over 20 years, died of a sud-den heart attack. The marriage had been extremely happy. Ken, a retired ordained minister, was Doe's dream man—intelligent, a gifted conversationalist, kind, a nifty Ascot-type dresser. By all accounts, he splashed Doe's consider-able private fortune around and they both enjoyed every minute of it. His sudden death shattered Doe.

Said Henry: "Sue needed more attention than people around her could really give her. We all knew Sue was having to deal with a lot, but Doe was also going through a time that was personally terribly difficult. Sue didn't seem to realize that other people had their own lives and had to continue with them despite her illness."

Henry's background was entirely different from Sue's. Henry was the only son of loving, supportive parents who gave their emotions free rein. His father was a Mexican-American, his mother Lebanese-American. He was raised to expect and delight in attention. Sue described him as very affectionate by nature, "a man who needed a lot of stroking."

Henry's family was one of inequality of power and authority between male and female. The father was the traditional household head; the mother provided all the domestic, parental and wifely comfort and support of the type that Sue could no longer provide. This cultural background was part of Henry's blood and bones. He was born in the United States and the influences of his family of origin had been modified by life's experiences, education and personal choice. Most men find it difficult to be an appendage to someone else's life, even that of their spouse, and Henry was no exception. On Cromarty Avenue, the Rodriguez household revolved around the woman. All the attention, all the public support, was for the woman.

Henry had come back home following Sue's diagnosis to be "a presence." He had not come home to be a nurse. He was clear about that in his own mind but Sue was not. However, as there was no nighttime help for the first year, and Sue had to be given her medication, taken to the bathroom and so on, Henry performed the role of caregiver with as much grace as he could. He did not resent doing it, but Sue was often critical about how he did it and acted as if he were there at her beck and call. He often arrived home from work exhausted, only to be up half the night looking after Sue. After a year, he felt he could not go on. He told Sue he had to get his sleep.

Said Sue: "He felt uncomfortable with illness, always had. The birth of Cole bothered him terribly. He couldn't stand to be there and developed headaches and was in the other room [during the birth]. He just has never been good at being a care-giver, or showing any sympathy when I've been ill."

Said Henry: "It wasn't that way at all. Cole's birth did *not* bother me. I even cut the umbilical cord! I am not a care-giver. But I am loving and caring. For a year [until May, 1993] we did not have night help. I did everything. I had to change her Kotex: I did that for a year. Once I grimaced: she was just so angry with me. There are some things that men don't want to deal with. I just felt I couldn't go on. I went to see Sandra Elder and she said we simply had to get night help. It's true I didn't want to get involved with Sue's care. She didn't seem to understand I didn't want my relationship on that level anymore. When I did try, at first, I couldn't do one thing right. I took Sue downtown one night to the theater. I'm trying to get the wheelchair in its proper place and she's telling me I'm doing it all wrong. I'd got her into the car, and driven downtown, and tried to do it properly. And all she did was criticize."

Said Sue: "I was terrified he'd tip me out, terrified I'd fall because he wouldn't hold me the way he was supposed to. I told him several times the right way to do it. He wouldn't listen to me."

Said Henry: "After that night, I all but gave up trying."

With Christmas over and the new year approaching,

Sue knew that she was entering a new stage. Every day now demanded that she relinquish some aspect of her privacy and independence. She endured these losses with good humor and entirely without shame or humiliation. The movement of her arms and hands, for example, was now so restricted that she could no longer wipe herself after going to the toilet. The home-maker did it for her. She did not experience this as a loss of dignity and accepted it with great simplicity. The dignity she sought to maintain was on a different level.

By now her periods had ceased entirely. That marked yet another shutting down of a life function, but she was happy about it. At the beginning of her illness, she had sought medical help to stop the monthly flow and its attendant nuisance factor. But the drug she'd used had had the opposite effect and she'd bled for months.

None of this bothered her. She spoke of these things with genuine amusement. She did not feel humiliated. She was totally at ease with her body and its functionings. This was a separate issue from the psychological pain caused by her total lack of mobility and the determination of strangers to tell her how she must die. When it came to having her bottom wiped, she was as simple and as fuss-free as a child.

These were the relationships, and this was the type of daily domestic situation in which Sue lived as she waited for her decision from the Supreme Court of British Columbia. Depicted publicly by her opponents as essentially self-indulgent and self-pitying, praised by her supporters as a hero, Sue sat in her wheelchair in the small ground-floor office which commanded a view of the garden and driveway, waiting alone, dying slowly, cared for only by strangers, destitute of the sustaining, unconditional warmth and love of a family.

There was, of course, a home-maker present in the kitchen, answering the phone, helping her take a bath, running the occasional message to get groceries, popping in to give Sue her medication or asking what she'd like for lunch. Her main daytime home-maker, Nadine Porter, came to be a friend, as did Chris Considine. Sharon Bartlett, the film producer, often went over to Vancouver Island to film events in Sue's life or simply to visit with her. Helma Libick frequently overnighted with Sue on weekends. The friend that gave her the greatest comfort was her new buddy, Svend Robinson, who phoned continually and visited often.

But there were times when Sue spent days devoid of any company except paid professionals, strangers all. It was a big house, furnished and carpeted in beige and lacking color and warmth. There was a silence and emptiness about it, and in it, Sue, in essence, was left to die alone. No one is blamed for this. Sue brought incredible courage and integrity to the dying process but she also brought a lot of unfinished family business—not only from her marriage but from her childhood. As she moved toward the end, the destructive effects of these unresolved conflicts became clear to her. But by then, weak, immobile and exhausted by speech, she could not resolve them. She accepted them with all the serenity she could muster, yet the failure to work them through eventually caused extreme grief and determined the timing she chose for her death.

It was no accident that Svend Robinson became a very particular friend. Since his election to Parliament 15 years earlier at the age of 27, he had associated himself with issues of social justice throughout the world. He had been publicly involved in issues of freedom and human rights in China, Russia, Bosnia-Herzogovina and South Africa, as well as in Canada. He was the first member in any high office in Canada to publicly acknowledge his homosexuality, a courageous move and one which has not adversely affected his popularity in his predominately blue-collar riding.

Loss of many friends in the gay community to AIDS had made Robinson supersensitive to the issue of terrible deaths. He had witnessed firsthand the destructive effects at every human level of prolonged and intense suffering and was already committed to assisted suicide when Sue went public. They were the same age. When they met, their mutual interest consolidated into a spontaneous, enduring and devoted friendship. Robinson, like Hofsess, saw Sue as a perfect vehicle to start a debate on a subject that he believed was decades overdue for a full public examination. But more than anything, Svend Robinson and Sue Rodriguez simply loved each other.

While Sue lacked for close personal company, she certainly did not want for professional help. The homemaker service—a woman during the day, another all night —was supplied by private agencies working under contract with the Capital Regional District (CRD) of Victoria. The CRD also supplied a physiotherapist, an occupational therapist and a visiting home nurse. There was Dr. Debbie Braithwaite, of the Victoria Hospice Society, and a hospice counselor, a speech therapist—who taught communication by blinking one's eyes until Sue asked her not to come back—a nurse and the family doctor. At one stage, Sue counted a total of 18 professionals involved directly with providing her care.

Sue was grateful but considered the system bureaucratic, wasteful and stressful. There was a constant turnover of home-makers over the months, which was exhausting. Sometimes their standards were simply unacceptable: one left morphine patches in the kitchen garbage where Sue's black-and-white spaniel, Oreo, could get at them, and dumped used surgical gloves on the kitchen counter. Endless paperwork surrounded everything—all of it for the patient's protection but adding nonetheless to an atmosphere of stress. When Sue's medication was changed, for instance—and as her illness progressed, the changes in morphine dosage were constant—the doctor would write the prescription and then inform the nurse who worked on Sue's case for the CRD. The nurse would call the pharmacy and fax the change to the home-maker agency. The nurse would then go to Sue's home and record the change in the hospice book kept in Sue's bedroom. If the nurse could not get to Sue's for several days, no agency employee, such as the home-maker, could give the new medication or even the new dosage of medication. If this change occurred on weekends, Sue had to manage without the drug that had been ordered unless there was a family member around to give it.

A network of strong, loving support would have reduced the stress and the depressing impact of being surrounded and cared for by strangers. More important, it would have mitigated Sue's feelings of aloneness and abandonment. That was not the reality.

When Mr. Justice Allen Melvin dismissed her application 12 days after hearing her case, Sue was disappointed and discouraged. But she was not surprised. She was learning the hard way what justice and law are all about. When she had originally decided to go to court, it was for herself. She hadn't been directly campaigning for other victims of terminal illness. She now realized that there was a whole hidden world of people dying in physical distress, loneliness and psychological pain, as she was.

After a few hours, and several long chats with Chris Considine, her disappointment passed. She felt her new-found inner strength reassert itself against the blow. She became conscious of the powerful force that existed deep within her, undisturbed by rejection and ready for war. She now had no doubts about the rightness of the path she had chosen. She decided to take that path to its utmost end. With a thrilling shock, she heard herself vowing: ". . . to the Supreme Court of Canada if necessary!"

Within the week, Sue had filed a notice of appeal.

Eight

The enormous social ramifications of the issues which Sue's application, and its subsequent denial, was addressing were not entirely skirted in Mr. Justice Allen Melvin's 22-page judgment. While he dealt almost entirely with the legal interpretations of Considine's arguments in relation to the Charter of Rights and Freedoms, Justice Melvin concluded with a forcible expression of opinion that touched directly on an issue that was—and will forever continue to be—at the heart of almost all law. And that is the good of the individual as opposed to the good of the greater society.

Most people assume that the courts are able to distinguish between what is fair and consequently "right," and what is unfair and consequently "wrong," and that legal procedure pursues fundamental justice. They go on to assume that the courts will issue compassion—or "justice"—for the physical, psychological and financial sufferings of individuals involved in court actions. But this is a naive notion. The courts do not dispense justice, they dispense law. The courts might, even in the majority of cases, dispense justice as the result of law. But the outcome depends on which lawyer interprets the law most accurately and persuasively to the satisfaction of the bench. Hence a constant tension exists between the law, which has been formulated to protect the majority of members in society, and the ideal of justice, which embraces fairness and compassion for society *and* individuals. In no aspect of law is this tension felt more strongly than in the question of assisted suicide and euthanasia.

Although this is *the* basic legal issue, there are others whose borders merge into a twilight zone of interrelating questions, such as public policy in a multicultural society, responsibility and self-determination, and who owns moral authority. Sue's cause demanded that society's attitudes towards death and dying be examined, and this demand was put out into a public arena in a society that has a variety of opinions about the existence of the soul, and that questions what is moral and what is not. When Sue said she did not understand Justice Melvin's point about protecting others, that "one has to be in the shoes of someone who is terminally ill to see what the real issue is," she was being perhaps naïve, but also existential. The very particular knowledge that she had acquired through her illness had the moral force of authenticity—and was juxtaposed with Melvin's concern for the vulnerable members of our society, which carried its own moral force.

The difficulties of extricating moral concerns from religious beliefs is another matter. It is fair to say, however, that there is general agreement that in a pluralistic secular society it is the law with its public policy implications, rather than any religious belief, that must be upheld. Because of this, an understanding of the law, as it relates to euthanasia and assisted suicide, is essential to any intelligent debate. The judgment of Justice Melvin touched on the relevant charter issues, and, as normally happens, these were developed and refined as the Rodriguez case went from one court to another.

His Lordship dismissed Section 241(b) of the Criminal Code (the law that makes aiding and abetting a suicide an indictable offense) as irrelevant to Sue's petition because it did not restrict or curtail Sue's freedom of choice or her ability to decide fundamental issues. It was her illness that deprived her of the opportunity to effectively carry out her wish, not the legal system nor the state.

Section 241(b) interfered with Sue's life, liberty and security of the person (he was referring to Section 7 of the charter) only to the extent that it interferes with the rights of others to assist Sue in committing suicide.

At this point, Justice Melvin pointed out a contingent issue. *If* Section 241 were struck on the basis that it violated Section 7 of the charter, Sue would have the right to request assistance at her suicide. However, the person who is so requested would have no duty at law to comply with her wishes. If it were otherwise, and such a duty existed which would be enforceable, it would ultimately mean Sue could apply for a court order to compel another person to assist her in committing suicide.

"When the petitioner's position is taken to that extreme, it demonstrates, in my view, that there is no right, as there is no corresponding duty," concluded Justice Melvin.

Regarding Section 7 of the Charter, which deals with the right to life, liberty and security of the person, His

Sue Shipley, 2, in 1952. Sue remembered her childhood as a happy time.

The Shipley family Christmas card photo, 1954. From left, Barbara, 6;
Tom Shipley II; Tom III, 3; Anne, 8 months; Dorothea Shipley; Sue, 4.

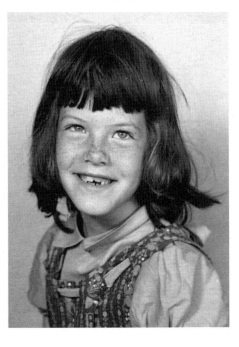

Sue at 6, in 1956.
Sue had a sense growing up
that she was "special." Both
her siblings and her aunt
agree that of all the Shipley
children, Sue stood apart;
they all felt she was destined
for something extraordinary.

As a teenager, Sue became rebellious. Doe and Tom were horrified to discover she was experimenting with drugs.

Sue's passport photo, 1967. She was 17, and ready to explore life. By 21 she'd been married and divorced and had moved to California.

Sue led an active, outdoor life, as these snapshots from her collection attest. Skiing in Utah and taking the sun in California were favorite pasttimes.

A strong, athletic woman with tremendous grace, Sue faced the terrible loss of what she considered to be her identity – her physicality – with ALS. "If I cannot move my own body I have no life."

Sue and Henry's wedding, 1981, in San Diego.

Sue with Cole, 1984 . . .

. . . 1987. After her
illness was diagnosed,
Sue became very
protective of her son.
He never appeared in
press photos.

The family rallies for Sue. From left, Sally, Anne, Tom, Sue, Barb, December, 1992. This was a rare display of support for Sue from her family. It was, it seemed, difficult for all of them to show real affection for one another. As Tom said, "Laziness plays a part in my family. We're also pretty inhibited."

Nick Didlick, *Vancouver Sun.*

Sue's legal battles brought her national attention. Here she is mobbed by press outside the B.C. Court of Appeal. One of her greatest strengths was her serenity, and even enthusiasm, in dealing with the press, as is obvious in this photo.

Lordship pointed out that these rights were subject to a limit—that the state could infringe on them if that infringement was in accord with fundamental justice. (Justice Melvin meant, for example, that people's liberty is infringed when they are put into prison, but putting them there is in accord with fundamental justice because criminals cannot be free to terrorize society.)

"Her fundamental decisions concerning her life are not restricted by the state," Justice Melvin said. "Her illness may restrict her ability to implement her decisions, but in my opinion, that does not amount to an infringement of a right to life, liberty or security of the person by the state."

Section 12 of the charter—everyone has the right not to be subjected to cruel or unusual treatment or punishment—was rejected as no punishment or treatment whatsoever was being imposed by the state. Nor was there any infringement of Section 15 of the charter—every individual is equal before and under the law—because Section 241(b) of the Criminal Code did not single out the disabled. The sanction applied equally to all persons, young and old, healthy and sick.

Mr. Justice Melvin also addressed two broader issues inherent in the Rodriguez application which he considered of grave importance. The first related to the question of the development of public policy, and here he quoted Mr. Justice Antonio Lamer, chief justice of the Supreme Court of Canada:

"The courts must not, because of the nature of the institution, be involved in the realm of pure public policy; that is the exclusive role of the properly elected representatives, the legislators. To expand the scope of Section 7 too widely would be to infringe upon that role."

Justice Melvin's second concern was also directed to Section 7 of the charter. The underlying hypothesis upon which the charter is based, he said, is the sanctity of human life. To interpret Section 7 so as to include a constitutionally guaranteed right to take one's own life as an exercise in freedom of choice is inconsistent with life, liberty and security of the person.

"Consequently, such a right to terminate one's life is not a constitutionally guaranteed right—and without such a constitutionally guaranteed right, the petitioner has no basis upon which to seek a remedy."

Justice Melvin concluded by coming out strongly in support of "the nature and purpose of Section 241, making those who assist suicide answerable to the law." Such a law was demonstrably justified in a free and democratic society. With the following words he aligned himself solidly with those who oppose any change to the status quo:

"It [Section 241] is designed to protect those who at a moment of weakness, or when they are unable to respond or unable to make competent value judgments, may find themselves at risk at the hands of others who may, with the best or with the worst of motives, aid and abet in the termination of life. Section 241 protects the young, the innocent, the mentally incompetent, the depressed and all those other individuals in our society who at a particular moment in time decide that termination of their life is a course that they should follow for whatever reason."

Justice Melvin's judgment, coupled with Sue's quick and determined retort that she'd fight it—"I really don't understand what he's talking about"—unleashed an emotional debate across the country. Open discussion on the right to suicide and its related question of euthanasia had been taboo. "Doesn't make good copy," newspaper editors had said. Now everyone had an opinion on the subject.

Interest in assisted death had been primed, particularly on the West Coast, by a controversial referendum in Washington State 14 months earlier. On November 5, 1991, Washingtonians were asked to vote on a proposition that would have legalized physician-assisted suicide as well as active euthanasia. Proposition 119, which was sponsored by the Hemlock Society, asked: "Shall adult patients who are in a medically terminal condition be permitted to request and receive from a physician aid-in-dying?" Aid-in-dying was described as "aid in the form of medical service, provided in person by a physician, that will end the life of a conscious and mentally qualified patient in a dignified, painless and humane manner, when requested voluntarily by the patient through a written directive . . . at the time the medical service is to be provided."

Albert Jonsen, a medical ethicist at the University of Washington Medical School, renowned for his temperate views, commented that the state of Washington was "on the edge of a moral cataclysm." Moral cataclysm or not, Proposition 119 was defeated by a vote of 54 to 46 percent.

At the same time as Justice Melvin's ruling, the Canadian Medical Association, representing 46,000 physicians, started a lengthy consultation with physicians on euthanasia-related issues. The association, which supports the criminal ban on euthanasia, said it would at least recommend changes to the general part of the core to clear up a perceived "chill" on doctors engaged in two common practices: withholding futile treatment of the terminally ill, and giving painkilling drugs to the dying even though such drugs might hasten death.

Editorials across the country widely supported Judge Melvin's ruling and applauded his position that it was Parliament, and not the courts, that should deal with the question. Anecdotal material poured into newspaper offices. There were letters and stories of death and dying with young and old, sometimes heroic, sometimes terrible, stories of suffering that went on interminably, and stories of unnamed doctors or friends who had helped, illegally, to put an end to suffering.

Svend Robinson denounced the New Democratic Party in Victoria for aligning itself—by virtue of defending an unjust federal law—with "right-to-life" forces. The Canadian Conference of Catholic Bishops (CCCB) entered the fray publicly for the first time on this issue. Categorizing the whole question as "a very public matter," the CCCB stated: "To accept killing as a private matter of individual choice is to diminish respect for human life, dull our consciences and dehumanize society." Marilyn Seguin of Dying With Dignity, who earlier had expressed some doubts about Sue's approach despite Seguin's organization's support of euthanasia, had no hesitation in responding. "The same old arguments," she said. "Who are these people to dictate to me that I do not have a right to make my own decision?" Hilda Kreig, of the Pro Life Society of British Columbia, summed up her feelings:

"The right to die really means reducing economic burdens of society, killing in the name of compassion, wanting Aunt Jane's inheritance sooner rather than later."

While this public debate continued in varying degrees of intelligence and acrimony, an emotional policy issue was splitting the 200-strong ALS community in Sue's home territory of Victoria. ALS Society board member Dr. Andrew Eisen, the man who had confirmed Sue's original diagnosis, called for a special meeting to try to mend the breach. The society's founder, Roy Slater (who has since died), and the executive director, Rhelda Evans, had, without leave of the society, publicly opposed Sue's fight to the point where they had submitted affidavits to bolster the case of the pro-life intervenors at the trial level. With the case going to the B.C. Court of Appeal, they were refusing to withdraw or rewrite them to remove any impression they were speaking on the society's behalf.

Dennis Kaye, British Columbia author of *Laugh, I Thought I'd Die* and ALS victim, said if the affidavits weren't withdrawn, the society could be destroyed. But Director Allan Graham told Sue and Hofsess that, although Evans and Slater were not authorized by the society to file their affidavits, he would not order them to withdraw them. He likely believed he'd be wasting his time.

Sue felt let down by her own. The affidavits, she said, depicted her as "a loser, a quitter . . . an eccentric and depressed individual making a weird request of the court." Any judge looking at them in future hearings would "see me falsely condemned by my peers."

Then Dr. Eisen himself added to the furor, not so much

within the society, but outside. The Rodriguez case had spread a lot of misinformation and shown a very "bleak and negative" view of ALS, he said. Although he did not name the affidavit of Dr. Donald Lovely, nor make a direct comment on Sue's testimony, there was no doubt as to Eisen's source of concern:

"It is virtually unheard of for someone with ALS to choke to death," he said. "It just doesn't happen. The vast number die quietly and peacefully in their sleep."

The renowned international specialist said that while many patients do progress to the ventilator stage, assisted suicide becomes a "non issue" at that point, because of the Nancy B. case. (Nancy B. was a 25-year-old Montreal woman suffering from Guillain-Barre syndrome, an incurable neurological disorder, who won the right in the Quebec Superior Court, January 1992, to have her ventilator disconnected.)

Sue felt let down by Dr. Eisen's statement, following as it did on the pro-life affidavits of Evans and Slater. Her disappointment remained private, shared with a few friends, one of whom was John Hofsess. But Hofsess decided to act.

A few days later, reporter Anne Mullens of the Victoria bureau of the *Vancouver Sun,* who had covered the Rodriguez story since it broke, was given a column by her editor and asked to rewrite it as a news story. The column, ostensibly from Sue Rodriguez, was signed with a shaky "S.R.," with the "R" trailing off as if the writer could not hold a pen. A letter, signed by Hofsess, accompanied the column: "Sue Rodriguez considers this issue to be extremely important to her and to others in British

Columbia with ALS. She has therefore drafted this commentary for your 'Voices' column and hopes very much it will be found worthy of publication."

Mullens was a seasoned and competent reporter. She had no reason to doubt the column's authenticity. She knew that Sue's hands were virtually useless and that Hofsess was a professional writer, so she assumed he had typed the piece. Hofsess had Mullens on his regular Right To Die Society fax list, and weekly, sometimes daily, sent her and other reporters across the country updates on developments in the legal challenge and on Rodriguez's health and progress. Sue, easily exhausted, had been satisfied with this arrangement. Mullens, knowing that Sue had had a bad week, declined to disturb her and confirmed the letter with Hofsess. She then wrote the story, which ran six columns wide across the front page of the news section.

"In a personal letter written to the *Vancouver Sun*, the Saanich woman lashed out at high-profile members of the ALS Society for opposing her court petition," Mullens wrote. "Said Rodriguez: 'Lately, I have come to realize that my illness is not the worst part of the ordeal I face [but] condemnation from the very society which is supposed to help people like myself. The ALS Society has done nothing but compound my misery.'"

Sue was on the phone to Mullens soon after the paper hit the streets denying any knowledge of the column and disassociating herself with the sentiments it expressed. Evans and Slater, she said, had a right to their opinion as individuals, just as she had a right to hers.

Devastated, Mullens contacted Hofsess. She was

stunned to hear him admit he had written the column, had not shown it to Sue, and yes, he had faked her signature.

Hofsess claimed that Sue had given her consent to the Right To Die Society to speak on her behalf. Sue had approved previous statements without changes, or with very minor ones. "You have to put it in its broadest context that Sue has reached a point in her disease where she cannot feed herself. It should come as no surprise to anyone that she does not write her own letters," he said in excuse.

Sue retorted angrily: "I am sick but I can still talk. No one talks for me but me." She emphasized that ALS Society members had been very helpful. President Phil Bissell had been "wonderful." She would never have criticized them.

The following day, Hofsess met with Sue at her home. That weekend Hofsess wrote a letter of apology both to Sue and the *Sun*. Hofsess said that because of his "over-zealousness" his actions had been "inappropriate and unethical." Sue's response was typical: "I don't want to make a big deal out of this and I don't feel a lot of anger. I want to put it behind us."

But the damage had been done. The right of self-determination, respect for a patient's autonomy, the need to recognize and respond to authenticity, had been the soul of Rodriguez's struggle. Her opponents had cried: it won't work that way; if euthanasia in any form is legalized there will be abuses; others will make decisions "for the good of" the voiceless, immobile terminally ill. And now Hofsess had bequeathed to them a brilliant example of their most fundamental argument. He had become the classic surrogate decision maker. He had decided what was the "best thing to do" for a terminally ill woman. He had not consulted her, had not said: "Is this what you want; is this how you really feel?" He had transferred his own views, his own needs, into the body of Sue Rodriguez and come up with a viewpoint and desire that reflected his values, his experiences, his understanding of the problems involved.

Hofsess's actions also confirmed another possibility: if religious pro-life individuals can adopt extreme, authoritarian attitudes toward "appropriate treatment" of terminal cases, so can pro-death individuals. Sue had retorted: "I am sick but I can still talk. No one talks for me but me." But had she not been able to say so, if she had no muscles in her throat and mouth, Hofsess could have gone on for months saying what he liked in her name.

The damage had also been done in the relationship between Sue and Hofsess. She knew Hofsess was perhaps her most devoted supporter. He had almost single-handedly opened up the right-to-die debate. Despite her wish to put the incident in the past, the sense of trust was gone. Sue said a year later: "To this day, although he admits it was a stupid mistake, he doesn't feel he did anything wrong." And so the whole affair died, its real significance examined, if in passing, only by reporter Anne Mullens, on whom the hoax had been played.

Bombarded by emotional stress and the increasing difficulty of doing even the most simple things, Sue sought to maintain her serenity and courage through reading. She found Elisabeth Kubler-Ross's *On Death and Dying*, a study of the psychological stages of dying, helpful. Now she read Gary Zukav's *The Seat of the Soul*, a mystical treatise on reincarnation and life after death.

One day, seated in the small office, thinking of the forthcoming hearing before the B.C. Court of Appeal, Cole bounced in and said he was going to build a snowman. Outside a fresh snowfall and a flash of sunlight had turned the grounds into a sparkling paradise. She felt full of love for this handsome boy, full of deep peace with the beauty of the world. "Build it in front of the window, where I can see," she said. Cole struggled into his jacket and boots, pulled a toque on his head and ran out. But he built the base of the snowman just out of Sue's range of vision. Too late he realized he could not move it; too late he realized his mother could not see it. Fumbling and struggling with her special chair that raised and lowered her from a seated or standing position, Sue felt a surge of pain and frustration. "And then I realized that it was there, the snowman was there, and Cole was happy building it. That is what really counted. It was going to be like that forever. He'd be doing so many things I would never see. The important thing was not that I saw it, but that he was happy doing in a world that, in the midst of a terrible winter, remained beautiful."

Nine

By the time Sue's case went to the B.C. Court of Appeal on February 15, 1993, the B.C. Coalition of People with Disabilities had joined the battle on her behalf and had been granted intervenor status.

The support of a coalition representing 800 disabled groups in British Columbia meant a great deal to Sue. In spite of the media attention, Sue's legal situation had remained totally unsupported by any group, with the exception of Hofsess's Right To Die Society. The only group with which she had been associated, the ALS Society, had voted finally to stay neutral after a deep division had split the ranks. Although there was a reasonable possibility that a basic discrimination against the disabled had been built into the law, Sue's had been the lone voice in demanding that the relevant section be struck.

The hearing before Chief Justice Allan McEachern and Justices Patricia Proudfoot and Bud Hollingrake opened on a frosty, sunny morning in Victoria before a courtroom of some 45 spectators. Sue, who had been battling a chest and throat infection, arrived with her home-maker, Nadine Porter, Svend Robinson and John Hofsess. Wrapped in a black coat, a bright red tartan blanket draped around her legs, Sue looked as optimistic and cheerful as she claimed to be.

Most of the main arguments that were to be presented over the next two days had already been heard at the trial level. However, the appeal process allows for development and refinement as well as new arguments, and as Considine led into the case, he was clearly on a new tack.

He boldly claimed that the lethal dose of medication that Sue required was merely a variation on recognized medical practices concerning terminally ill or vegetative patients. He argued that under existing common law, dying patients had a number of options for managing the terminal stages of their life. They could accept drugs or machines to prolong life, could refuse them or could revoke permission for the continuance of life-sustaining measures they were already receiving.

Considine also referred to a normal standard of practice in palliative care—giving patients with intractable pain enough drugs to stop the pain, even though the dose is so high it kills them.

Chief Justice McEachern was so singularly unimpressed with Considine's argument that physician-assisted suicide could be characterized as palliative care, that he told opposing counsel to ignore it in their responses. He informed Considine that if he was to succeed at all, it could only be under the charter.

Sue listened intently as Considine, after pausing respectfully for the chief justice's mild rebuke, rebounded with an argument that Mr. Justice Melvin had erred because he had based his conclusion partly on the finding that a physician has no duty to assist a suicide.

"It is a matter of personal conscience for a physician," he said. Ms Rodriguez either had to kill herself while she was still enjoying life or else "she will be forced to participate in an illegal act." If she did not kill herself, and if no one was legally permitted to kill her, then she would be forced to endure intrusive medical treatment, or slowly starve to death while fully cognizant of her situation.

This was a new approach to Considine's earlier charter argument that Sue had "the right to commit suicide" or "the right to live her life with dignity," which in this case meant the right to choose the time and manner of her death.

Denying a person this right, and forcing them into an illegal act or the act of starvation, was a violation of Section 7 of the charter, Considine said. One remedy, he concluded, would be to leave Section 241 as it was, but for the court to grant Sue Rodriguez an exemption so that she could have a physician-assisted suicide with impunity; any future applicants would be dealt with separately.

The B.C. Coalition of People with Disabilities then presented its case: as the objective of the coalition is to ensure that the Criminal Code does not prevent the mentally competent who are disabled from exercising their rights, the basis of the arguments put forward by Coalition lawyers James Pozer and James Sayre dealt with unequal treatment and the necessity of autonomy. At the same time, Pozer emphasized that the coalition did not promote death or favor suicide, and was not saying that a disability is a valid or appropriate reason for taking one's life.

"Able-bodied people in Canada can attempt suicide as long as they act on their own," said Pozer. "This is true whether they are incompetent, mentally ill, unduly influenced or coerced. However, mentally competent people with physical disabilities who are unable to commit suicide on their own—short of starving themselves—are deprived of the right of self-determination and autonomy, freedom of choice and control of their body."

The decision to commit suicide was a fundamental personal decision which the law indirectly prevented the disabled, but not the able-bodied, from exercising. Therefore, Section 241 of the Criminal Code violated Section 15 of the charter.

Ace Henderson, like Considine, had also polished his arguments. He did not dispute the fact that the code had a "disparate effect" on the physically disabled but it could not be defined as discrimination:

"It is true that the disabled are prevented from doing something others can do, but it is not discrimination in the context that it does not confer a benefit or advantage, or impose a burden on one group or another," Henderson claimed. The law was "a reasonable and necessary limit" to a person's freedom, under the charter, to protect the vulnerable. It should not be changed.

Outside the courtroom, one of the spectators who had weathered the protracted arguments in their entirety, paused to make a provocative statement. Dr. Scott Wallace, a retired physician, a former member of the Legislative Assembly and former leader of the B.C. Progressive Conservative party, said that he had not spoken to Sue but that he would consider helping her to commit suicide.

"I've listened to the trial and the appeal and I'm most

disappointed at the way the courts go on as if we're deal-ing with a motor car engine that can't be fixed," he said. "If I were asked, well, I'd consider it. But I haven't been asked. I'm certainly not offering. It's the last thing I would feel compelled to do. But, I'd consider it."

Dr. Wallace, prominent in British Columbia politics for a generation, is a medical consultant to the Right To Die Society of Canada. He said he'd been wrestling with the issue of Sue's request for some time.

"Your head tells you that it's against the law, you mustn't do it, and it can lead to misunderstanding of a doctor's role in society by doing something that has just legally never been considered before," Wallace said. "On the other hand, anybody that has any kind of heart just has to look at the kind of future that Sue Rodriguez faces and you're bound to feel that someone should show some basic human compassion."

Justice McEachern had promised an early decision, but during the following three weeks as she waited, Sue was continuously active, the last period of such intense activ-ity in her life. Although her ability to speak, swallow and walk was measurably deteriorating, she felt well, was without pain and was confident that her message was not only reaching a large audience but was being understood. In sharp contrast to her sense of public well-being was her increasing private despair.

At home the small but sharp tensions that asserted themselves whenever she and Henry tried to do anything together, or even to discuss anything together, remained. Neither was disposed to create scenes, but the household, where quiet and respectful standards of ordinary manners dominated, was awash with unspoken turmoil. Sue had understood intellectually that Henry had slipped away from her, but only now was she beginning emotionally to assimilate it, to understand that she had absolutely no ability to bring him back. For a while she had not wanted to, had been content to have him around as a companion, but this ability, even desire, to let go of him had not survived the terrible needs for a personal, intimate recognition and relationship that arose within her as a direct result of her illness.

All her life Sue had enjoyed that particular combination of intelligence, physical energy and quick wit that makes for true attractiveness. Her cousin Anna Sweeny described her as being "brainy and beautiful, both as a little girl and a woman." Anna, the sole survivor of the tragic childhood fire that killed her mother and three siblings, lives in Connecticut but has always kept in contact with Sue. "She was very physically capable and strong, with an impish, mischievous wit," said Anna. "I'd always thought of her as the outstanding one in the whole clan. And, as it turned out, I was right."

Sue had now lost these lifelong physical attributes, not slowly as one does with age, but virtually overnight. Week by week her body was turning into that of a stranger. Severe illness desexualizes a person and robs them of the comfort and confidence that goes with awareness of sexual power. This was another reality that Sue faced: the power that she had grown up with as a female was gone. That is a terrible loss. All women experience it—but not overnight, and not at 42.

Sue would later say: "I have never been a strongly sexual person, never really had a strong need for sex. Affection has always been far more important to me." The need of human beings to appear attractive, to be lovable in the sight of those we love, particularly of the opposite sex, is a different matter. Sue's need for this personal affection was undiminished by illness, and had probably increased. Henry could give admiration, support and friendship. His support of Sue's legal battle was unfailing. But he could not play the role of lover, not even psychologically. He had, as he said, his own integrity.

Sue was not aware at this time that even their tenuous friendship was being placed in jeopardy by the complexities of their personal needs, needs which were being heightened by the crisis they were living through. Henry was beginning to wonder if there was any point in persisting in his attempts at friendship, beginning to wonder if he should not give himself permission to find a girlfriend. He would later say: "My struggle to remain a friend was intense and difficult. For a year and a half after I returned home, I tried every day to be a strong and loyal friend. I saw no one else, went nowhere else, except perhaps to a neighbor's for coffee, and that would be just to get out of the house and have a little time to myself. All I asked was for me to be myself, but she wouldn't allow it."

There were other stresses to be managed. Their main concern was Cole, who had started to have nightmares and would awake screaming. Sue could no longer get out of bed to go to him, had to lie there until Henry heard and went and took the child into his arms and soothed him back to sleep. In the dark she would weep at her helplessness, her inability to make her frozen body move, to fly down the hall, hold the child, kiss his fears away. The pain of this deprivation was physical: she once described it as being like a hot spot at the back of her neck, a strangling weight in her lungs.

She and Henry had painstakingly explained to Cole what the legal struggle was all about. "I do not ever want to leave you," she had said, "but I have a disease that's not curable right now, and I'm going to get weaker, and probably eventually die." She had told him that the very first night after her diagnosis, a decision that she and Henry had taken together. Later, she had told him how she wanted to die: "I want to leave you while I am still happy, still enjoying the life that I have. I do not want to suffer for a long time and I do not want you and Dad to have to watch me suffering. When that happens, I want a doctor to help me to die. And I want the law to let me do it because it is wrong to break the law."

Now, once a week after school, Cole spent an hour with a counselor who carefully prepared him to handle the confusion, fear and grief that would accompany his mother's death. He first went to the school counselor for this, and later to a Victoria Hospice Society group for children whose parents had died or were dying.

Despite the "night terrors," as Sue called them, a positive change in Cole's attitude and understanding had occurred. His need for his mom to be like the other mothers of his classmates had once been desperate. Being a normal little boy, he had hated her difference, hated the big, bulky wheelchair that got between his body and hers, hated her useless legs, hated her strange and difficult speech. Cole had hated these things with all the wild grief of an eight-year-old, soon-to-be-motherless child. But this initial anger had dissipated under the glow of her new fame. He had been surprised to find that, whenever his mother was in public, strangers would smile at her, little groups would clap as her wheelchair moved by, people would shout from passing cars: "Good luck, Sue." It was embarrassing but he couldn't help but feel proud that his mom was so special, so important. Now at night he often saw his mom on television. Later, as Sue's deterioration and imminent death weighed on his child's heart, his attitude would revert to confusion and pain. But for the time being, all was well.

These problems at home were not the only difficulties. The question of Sue's mounting legal costs begged an immediate solution. John Hofsess's Right To Die Society had funded Sue's court actions, but was already $55,000 in debt and facing a $10,000 debt if the case went to the Supreme Court. In an effort to raise funds, Vancouver actor-director Russell Roberts held a fund-raising night for Sue at Victoria's McPherson Theatre with a reading of the play, *Whose Life Is It Anyway?*, by British playwright Brian Clark. On the same day as the reading—which raised $1,700—Sue was named the first Canadian Humanist of the Year by the Humanist Association of Canada. This is a national organization of atheists and agnostics founded by Dr. Henry Morgentaler and linked to the American Humanist Society.

And then, on March 8, the decision came down. By a vote of two to one, the B.C. Court of Appeal turned down Sue's application.

Ten

March 8, 1993

Sue reacted calmly to the defeat: "I am getting weaker and can feel myself deteriorating. Another delay makes me feel anxiety. But I am committed to continuing."

Sue's determination was well based. While Justices Proudfoot and Hollingrake voted against the appeal, the formidable chief justice McEachern had voted in her favor. So powerful and supportive was the Chief Justice's judgment that Considine and Sue decided immediately to proceed to the Supreme Court of Canada. Chris Considine said that, because of the importance of the issue, he would relinquish all legal fees.

Madam Justice Proudfoot's denial rested on two precise issues. One was that Sue would not be the one punished under the Criminal Code Section 241(b), so her application in effect sought to excuse an unnamed person from future criminal liability. There was, said Justice Proudfoot, no legal authority or precedent that she was aware of that would allow for this. The second issue concerned the proper role of the courts in the matter of liberalizing laws relating to euthanasia. The court could not assess the consensus of Canada on the issue. It was up to Parliament to make such public policy decisions.

Mr. Justice Hollingrake agreed. He said that sometimes the courts could be validly criticized from shying away from the full force of the power entrusted to them under the charter. But in an area that involved philosophical rather than legal issues, and where public opinion was polarized, Parliament should decide.

In Justice Hollingrake's judgment, Sue's right of "security of the person" *was* infringed according to concepts of human dignity already acknowledged in previous cases. However, Section 7 was *not* breached because the infringement was allowable—that is, in accord with the principles of fundamental justice. These principles are formed by all the values in society—legislative, social and philosophical. The legislature had never recognized assisted suicide as being part of the values most people in society adhered to.

Justice Hollingrake said that he had reviewed legislative history, including decriminalization of suicide in 1972, and a report from the Law Reform Commission of Canada, Working Paper No. 28 (1982) on euthanasia and aiding suicide, and this had convinced him that physician-assisted suicide had never been accepted by Parliament or the medical profession.

He urged the courts to exercise caution in using the charter as a tool for social reform. Before the courts intervened in society's life, he concluded, there must be a medical, legislative or societal basis for doing so. As this basis did not exist in the Rodriguez case, he could not support the application.

Chief Justice Allan McEachern expressed "profound

misgivings about almost every aspect of this case," yet there was no reflection of any misgivings in his resolute tone of judgment.

This judgment was of an altogether different nature and dimension to that of Justices Hollingrake's or Proudfoot's. Justice McEachern acknowledged at length medical reports that described Sue's physical condition and the demeaned quality of life awaiting her before she died. This was an interesting inclusion because it recognized an existential dimension that touched on very difficult-to-define areas of justice and philosophy. Although this existential dimension—in this case Sue's personal experience—is as real as any other consideration, it often has no place in law.

Justice McEachern was stating that Sue's reality was such that Section 241(b) offended her charter rights under Section 7. To support his argument, Justice McEachern quoted the same paper that Justice Hollingrake had used to deny Sue's application, but used a different section:

"In its 1982 Working Paper No. 28, the [Law Reform] commission stopped just short of recommending the 'decriminalization' of assisted suicide because of concern about abuse. But then it stated: 'At the same time, in order to acknowledge more fully the undeniable element of altruism and compassion involved in some cases of assistance provided to a terminally ill loved one, and because we are not convinced that the imposition of a criminal sentence is appropriate in such a case, the commission proposes a second subsection to the Criminal Code as follows: No person shall be prosecuted for an offense under the present section without the personal written authorization of the attorney general.'"

Said Justice McEachern: "In my judgment, the intention was that assisted suicide of terminally ill persons would be effectively decriminalized because it was expected that the attorneys general would not give authorization to prosecute such cases."

From this, Chief Justice McEachern understood that the commission was sympathetic to the decriminalization of assisted suicide, but was not able to develop adequate safeguards against abuse.

The chief justice then pointed out that the charter was enacted in 1982 and Criminal Code Section 241 was enacted in 1892. Justice McEachern's point was that during that century there had been a radical shift in many of society's values and understandings.

He then quoted the 1991 Seaton Report from the British Columbia Royal Commission on Health Care and Costs: "The principle which has guided us in our deliberations is that, wherever possible, the person who is dying should have the right to determine the form and time of death. Respecting this will help ensure a dignified death."

After discussing the situation in the Netherlands, where unofficial and official euthanasia has been practiced for some time "to the extent that an estimated 25,000 people die at the hands of physicians annually," Chief Justice McEachern judged that Section 241 violated Sue's rights under Section 7 of the charter. These two issues were related in that the chief justice believed there was a widespread desire for physician-assisted suicide and that with the proper safeguards in place, it would be legally and socially acceptable.

Justice McEachern set out six conditions as a remedy for the case before him. If these conditions were strictly complied with, neither Sue nor any physician assisting her to die, would commit any offense against the law of Canada.

First, Sue must be mentally competent to make a decision to end her own life. This competence was to be certified in writing by her doctor (that is, any doctor willing to do it) and by an independent psychiatrist who had examined Sue not more that 24 hours before "final arrangements" were put into place (that is, an intravenous machine set up with a fatal dose, whatever the method to be used). Such an "arrangement" must be operative only when Sue's doctor is present with her. This written certificate must include an opinion of competency, and the belief that Sue truly desired to end her life, and had reached this decision of her own free will without any outside influence.

Second, the physicians must certify that: a) Sue is terminally ill and near death and has no hope of recovering; b) that she is, or but for medication would be, suffering unbearable physical pain or severe psychological distress; c) that she is aware she has a continuing right to change her mind; and d) when, in their opinions, Sue would likely die if palliative care is being administered to her, or if palliative care should not be administered to her.

Third, not less than three days before Sue is examined by a psychiatrist for the purpose of preparing the required certificate, notice must be given to the regional coroner, and the coroner or his nominee (who must be a physician) may be present at the examination of Sue by the psychiatrist. This would be to ensure that Sue had the mental competence to decide to terminate her life.

Fourth, Sue must be reexamined each day after the certificate has been issued to ensure she has not changed her mind.

Fifth, if the certificate is not exercised within 31 days after issuance, it becomes invalid.

Sixth, the act actually causing Sue's death must be her own unassisted act and not the act of someone else.

Chief Justice McEachern's judgment was only one of three, and it failed. Sue was discovering that the role of law is not that of benevolent social care-giver; nor does it provide sanctuary for personal suffering—although Justice McEachern's judgment would have had it so, given the larger implications of her suit. Sue's pain did not, in the end, concern the court, only the legal ramifications of her fight to die. This distance from human reality gives the court the necessary objectivity to interpret the law equitably, but it can also diminish the importance of the unique issue at hand—in Sue's case, what degree of suffering should a person have to endure for the hypothetical protection of the rest of society? It was this distance between written law and constantly changing human reality—noted in Justice McEachern's statement that much has changed since the Criminal Code was set down in 1892—that Justice McEachern bridged in his judgment.

Such a judgment by the chief justice of the appeal court of a Canadian province would have been inconceivable even a decade ago. It reflected the fact that Sue's legal struggle had far broader implications than the personal battle of a dying woman for the right to determine the timing of her own death. Justice McEachern's judgment mirrored the times, just as Sue's application did—times when the meaning of life is being reinterpreted, when people's visions of the world have shifted and in many cases shattered. Uncertainty and doubt about the value and the function of society's dominant institutions is widespread. A pressing need to challenge the authority of these institutions has resulted. Sue's stance was part of that and so was Justice McEachern's judgment.

Perhaps the most significant social changes have occurred in the medical community. For centuries, life and death had been thought Nature's or God's business. The ability of the lungs to breathe, the heart to pump, the muscles to move, was generally believed to be a matter of fate, of God's will, of a cosmic plan. Almost overnight, medical technology could stop or start any of that—could, in fact, maintain a life, which appeared to be devoid of any meaning or quality, for an indefinite number of years; a life which, without such intervention, would simply and naturally pass on. To many in the aging population, the possibility of lingering interminably is more frightening than the approach of a doctor with a deadly cocktail.

At the other end of the spectrum, displacing God or chance or fate or Nature were the medical geneticists, targeting part of inherited life chains and engineering physical and mental capacities of the yet-to-be-born. Or the laboratory worker, with no relationship whatsoever to the egg's mother or the sperm's father, starting a human life at will in a laboratory test tube, then planting it in a human uterus or deep-freezing it or flushing it down the drain. People who thought they knew what life was all about, and where they stood in the universal scheme of things, were no longer sure.

On a more mundane level, the relationship between patient and doctor has also changed. Doctors were once part of the sacred structures of society, part of a hierarchy of authority that—with the exception of the judicial system—is now almost totally rejected. Paradoxically, despite this rejection, an archetypal image of doctors as beings with godlike healing qualities lingers. People's attachment to this image, despite a cultural climate in which suits for malpractice have become commonplace, still remains strong enough to produce resentment when reality intervenes. Their adulation of those who may ultimately have the power of life or death has become a cause for resentment, now that trust is widely corroded. Nothing is certain any longer.

Sue had moved intuitively into this climate of uncertainty and become the carrier of an idea that had been gaining momentum among all groups, but particularly among those who grew into adulthood in the sixties and seventies. She was unconsciously acknowledging that there is no longer any socially based philosophical consensus about life or death. Further, she personally was unwilling to allow the medical, legal or theological professions to adopt a paternalistic attitude toward her life or her death. Her court action was a claim on her right to be responsible for those experiences herself. To do that, she had challenged the law to redefine and restructure itself in relation to many of society's most powerful institutions.

Whether for good or for bad, that essentially was what Sue's struggle was about, and why, when the appeal court decision was announced on March 8, 1993, its majority decision was nationally regarded as being of profound significance—almost as significant as the stunning dissenting opinion of the province's chief justice.

The media was not the only group analyzing and tracking every move and argument in the Rodriguez case. Across Canada and in the United States there was mounting concern among widely diversified religious groups and organizations for the handicapped, at the direction the case was taking, the issues that were being raised and the issues that were not being raised. By now only one thing was clear: on the matter of assisted suicide, there was no unanimity.

Eleven

March to May 1993

On the same day that the B.C. Court of Appeal turned down Sue's request for a physician-assisted suicide, Svend Robinson announced that an unidentified doctor had contacted Sue at home and offered to give her whatever was required to kill her when the time came—regardless of the consequences.

(Robinson later said he had been at Sue's home with this doctor—Dr. Michael Priest—when Chris Considine phoned to say that the appeal had been turned down. Soon after, Robinson with Sue, John Hofsess and Dr. Priest went into Victoria for a press conference at Considine's office. "We let [Dr. Priest] off before arriving to protect him," said Robinson. "This doctor did a lot of international humanitarian work and was finally unable to help because he was out of the country." A second doctor had then come forward, met with Sue, but was unable "for personal reasons" to assist.)

Robinson did this despite Considine's strong objection. Considine, the soul of propriety, was aghast at the political maneuvering. He wanted to be associated only with legal issues and not with what could appear to be a radical group meddling in illegal death.

It was a week for letting everything hang out. A few

days later John Hofsess went one better than Robinson. He announced that not one, but probably two doctors would help Sue commit suicide. It would be done in public and there would be no attempt to cover up. He said that his Right To Die Society had found the doctor, or doctors, and was actively seeking others. "Everyone would be on hand" at Sue's death, he said, presumably meaning himself, the doctor or doctors and Svend Robinson. "The more people present, the stronger the message that is sent to government. We can't pin our hopes on one doctor."

Considine didn't like even a peripheral association with any of this. He phoned Hofsess at home and told him so. Sue didn't appreciate it either. The announcement was a replay of the earlier faked letter incident, with Hofsess speaking on her behalf without a by-your-leave.

"I deeply regret that John has made statements concerning my life which are both inaccurate and made without consultation with me," she said.

This statement came in a news release, issued from Robinson's Vancouver riding office, in which she severed all ties with the Right To Die Society. Robinson, the society's political consultant, also cut his ties. Later, in Ottawa, Robinson told a press conference that Hofsess had violated a fundamental principle—Sue's right to speak for herself. He then referred to the letter-writing incident: "It is not the first error in judgment made on that principle."

Hofsess was devastated.

"It pains me beyond measure to hear [they] are severing their ties," he said. "It appears that I have become a scapegoat in an expedient political maneuver designed to make sure that future news about Sue is more strictly controlled by those who advise her."

Sue had become a hot political property in the right-to-die movement. She felt no particular hesitancy in dumping Hofsess, even though his efforts had turned her into a national figure, and even though he had devoted ten years of his life to the same cause she was fighting for. Sue's awareness of the political aspects of her struggle had developed considerably since she first went to court under Hofsess's aegis. She now believed Hofsess "would accomplish nothing because he does things in a way that is unacceptable to society." Robinson, unlike Hofsess, was direct and aggressive in his approach, both personally and politically, and as well had had 15 years in Parliament to hone his political skills and connections. She now saw in Robinson, as he clearly saw in her, the possibilities of an effective political alignment. Together, they moved Hofsess out of their territory.

An effective political alignment was going to be essential if the right-to-die movement was to succeed. On March 22, less that a week after this affair, members of Parliament overwhelmingly rejected a private member's motion proposed by New Democrat Ian Waddell (Port Moody, Coquitlam) that would have required the government to "consider the advisability of introducing legislation" on euthanasia.

This motion would not have changed the law. It would have merely required the government to examine the issue. Nonetheless, it lost 140 to 25. At precisely the same time, the Angus Reid poll indicated 76 percent of Canadians supported patient-requested euthanasia, and 70 percent believed physician-assisted suicide should be legally permitted. These results suggest one of two things: that politicians are totally out of touch with the values of those who elect them, or that the questions posed in the poll were not sufficiently fine-tuned to elicit a precise reading of national sentiment. As this issue is not about to die, time will provide the answer.

On March 29, Chris Considine was notified that the Supreme Court of Canada had set aside one day, May 20, to hear the Rodriguez case. The Supreme Court was immediately "bombarded," according to one source, with requests for intervenor status. Sue, true to form, found this amusing and amazing: "Why on earth would anyone want to impose their own value system on me? I've got mine, they've got theirs."

Intervenor status was granted to five organizations in addition to the two that had already appeared at the trial or appeal levels—the B.C. Coalition of People with Disabilities, and the Pro Life Society of British Columbia and Pacific Physicians for Life Society. The five new intervenors were Dying With Dignity; the Right To Die Society of Canada; Coalition of Provincial Organizations of the Handicapped (now called the Council of Canadians with Disabilities); Canadian Conference of Catholic Bishops and the Evangelical Fellowship of Canada; and People in Equal Participation Inc.

The Canadian Conference of Catholic Bishops said the case "raises some of the most profound moral, legal and social issues that any court or any civilized society can ever be called upon to make." The Ottawa press gallery asked that the proceedings be televised. This was agreed to for only the second time in Canada's history.

The actual hearing at the Supreme Court of Canada in Ottawa is essentially a formality, if a critical one. Months before the court meets (in Sue's case it was only weeks, the process accelerated due to her physical condition), every intervenor receives the arguments of all other intervenors in the same case. The real argument of an intervenor is done in writing in a factum, which is then filed in Supreme Court weeks in advance of the hearing. By the time the court sits, the judges are familiar with all arguments and have had considerable time in which to ponder the issues. It is then a matter of the petitioner and each intervenor giving a summary of their arguments, and the justices posing any questions that remain unanswered from their reading of the factums.

Everyone must be well organized and precise. The intervenors are allowed 15 minutes, the petitioner—in this case Considine—is allowed one hour.

Early on the morning of Thursday, May 20, 1993, Sue settled into a big soft chair in the basement rec. room of her Saanich home awaiting the arrival of the press—for the "zoo-rama" as she called it. By eight a.m. the room was crowded with reporters, photographers and TV cameramen leapfrogging one another in an effort to get the best shot of this woman who, virtually single-handedly, had managed to bring one of the most pressing and controversial issues of the day onto the nation's top judicial agenda. For Sue, it was a day of triumph. Had her health allowed, she would have gone to Ottawa to witness the event firsthand. She had considered it, but her doctor warned that her breathing would be dangerously stressed by the flying, and exposure to common viruses, such as flu, could have fatal results. She had no desire to choke to death on a plane, so she stayed at home.

The hearing in Ottawa got under way with an impressive decorum that was far removed from the near scrum a short while earlier in the barristers' room, where some fifteen barristers struggled in limited space to gown themselves for this historic event without putting an elbow into the ribs of their fellow intervenors. Security was incredibly tight. All briefcases and files were surveyed by metal detectors on arrival at the building, and, once gowned, lawyers were again stopped and searched as they went into the courtroom.

The stress that accompanies appearing before the Supreme Court was higher than usual this day because the entire proceedings were to be televised nationally. However, the televising turned out to be totally unobtrusive. Two fixed cameras, like little round eyes, were set on the bench, one to film the intervenor, another to capture the scarlet-clad judges.

The importance of Sue's case was obvious from the full lineup of nine judges. Nine is ideal, five is the minimum. Work loads or illness sometime force the court to go with seven. The courtroom itself is comparatively small, holding perhaps 100 people. On this day, one-third of those present were lawyers, and the rest were reporters, with only a handful of the public.

Sue watched the proceedings intently, with little change of expression as it moved smartly along. It was clear from the questions asked that the bench was well prepared and had given a great deal of thought to the issue. On the CBC, the hearing was interspersed with a documentary on Sue's life at home—Sue sipping from a glass held by Nadine, Sue, held upright, shuffling slowly from the bathroom to her recliner chair. Watching it, Sue said it was "weird" to see herself on the screen. The conjecturing by various intervenors as to her life expectancy was hard to take.

The arguments of Considine, the B.C. Coalition of People with Disabilities (represented by James Pozer and James Sayre) and the Pro Life Society of British Columbia and Pacific Physicians for Life Society (represented by Ace Henderson and Neil Milton) were the same as they had been in the B.C. Court of Appeal, with one exception. Considine included a request that the court impose "a set of limiting conditions." These conditions were virtually identical with those presented by Chief Justice McEachern.

The government—Johannes Van Iperen and James D. Bissell for the attorney general of Canada, and George Copley for the attorney general of British Columbia—defended the constitutionality of the laws it had enacted.

The complexity of the issue, the fact that it dealt with moral, spiritual, social and cultural dimensions as well as the immediate problem of profound human suffering, was well recognized in most of the interventions. They were by and large a balancing act between profound compassion for Sue's situation and a need to act, and a recognition of the potential for abuse and the difficulties of guaranteeing effective procedural safeguards. The polarization that characterizes public debate on the issue was absent. A clear recognition that Parliament, not the court, should be dealing with the issue ran through each intervention.

Dying with Dignity, for instance, intervened in support of Sue but were not shy about talking of "the sanctity of life" which some pro-assisted-suicide and euthanasia groups regard as a cliché. Martin Campbell argued that respecting the right of the individual to make personal choices enhances life's value and sanctity. It was essential to preserve the sanctity of life: that sanctity includes the right to make fundamental personal decisions. On the other hand, Dying with Dignity was not convinced that Section 7 of the charter (right to life, liberty and security of the person) included a right to commit suicide—as a right to make personal decisions—without interference from the state. Furthermore, it did not advocate the removal of Criminal Code Section 241 "unless supervision would be put into place to protect the vulnerable."

In supporting Sue, Campbell asked for an exemption in her case: the individual circumstances of a single patient shouldn't necessarily be a template for all people in all circumstances. He argued—as Dying with Dignity has done consistently over the years—that Parliament, not the court, was "the appropriate body to resolve the religious, moral, ethical, social and legal issues which arise in amending the prohibition against assisted suicide in the context of a person near death."

As Parliament would not resolve the issue in the time left for Sue, compassion demanded an exemption be made. So Campbell sought a recommendation from the court to the attorney general of British Columbia that criminal proceedings should not be started against a physician who helped Sue die as long as certain criteria (to be set by the court) were met. The criteria would likely be similar to that set out in the appeal court minority decision of Chief Justice Allan McEachern.

Next was Robyn M. Bell (with John Laskin) representing John Hofsess's Right To Die Society of Canada. Bell sought a declaration that Section 241 was unconstitutional, therefore invalid. He argued that Section 241 infringed on Section 7 by "infringing on the security of the person by taking away mental and physical integrity; infringed on a person's liberty by taking away autonomy in making decisions; and infringed on life through removing dignity from the quality of life."

The intervention of the Coalition of Provincial Organizations of the Handicapped (COPOH) provided the best example of the complexities of the issue. COPOH is a national umbrella organization that represents 163 organizations, with a membership of 75,000. Although COPOH technically intervened against Sue because its arguments focused on safeguards to protect the vulnerable, it actually supported her.

Acting for COPOH, Anne Molloy argued that the Criminal Code Section 241 violated Sue's charter rights under Section 15 (equality) because its effect was to discriminate against the disabled. She sought a constitutional exemption that Section 241 would not apply in cases where a person with a physical disability required help to suicide. She then proposed specific safeguards to protect the vulnerable.

Molloy, a lawyer for the Advocacy Resource Center for the Handicapped (ARCH) in Toronto—a legal aid clinic that specializes in precedent-setting cases involving disability rights—is, at 40, a veteran Supreme Court intervenor. She later explained COPOH's complicated position.

"We were deeply concerned about the implications of the B.C. Court of Appeal decision. This decision essentially said that it was not legislation that prevented Sue from committing suicide, it was her disability itself. That could be said about every disabled case and therefore there would be no discrimination. But most discrimination against people with disabilities arises from failure to accommodate their needs.

"We were also very concerned that there be a disabled voice that showed both sides of the picture, a coalition that could put forward the pros and cons of assisted suicide. So most of our factum pointed out how vulnerable the disabled were and that they needed protection from their lives being devalued. We wanted safeguards there to make sure people are not taken advantage of or pressured into doing something they didn't want to do. People can be influenced by a doctor or relative saying: 'Don't live on a respirator, that would be sheer hell.' But how do they know, if they haven't done it themselves? Maybe it's better than being dead. Some in the medical profession, and some families, subtly encourage the disabled to quit fighting.

"COPOH wanted the court to know it was aware of these dangers but that it felt people's competent wishes should be respected. We were reinforcing the right to chose. The safeguards were okay in this case—Sue had met them—and we supported her individual remedy."

The Canadian Conference of Catholic Bishops (CCCB) joined with the Evangelical Fellowship of Canada (EFC) for their opposing intervention. The CCCB—with 75 dioceses and 11.4 million Catholics—was founded in 1943 to bring "moral, philosophical and spiritual perspective" to policy and social issues. The EFC comprises 28 Protestant denominations, which represent Canada's 2.5 million evangelicals. When the whole issue is debated and voted on in Parliament—as Sue's fight has made inevitable—this combination will constitute a powerful opposition to any attempt to liberalize current prohibitions against assisted suicide and euthanasia.

Robert Nelson, on behalf of this alliance, opposed Sue on two grounds. One was religious—the so-called God-card. This was a risky card to play. The charter guarantees freedom of religion, so unless all religions have the same view of suicide, it's difficult to make a case that it's against the law simply because Christianity forbids it. Nelson quoted the preamble to the charter—"Whereas Canada is founded on principles that recognize the supremacy of God and the rule of law"—and argued that physician-assisted suicide is contrary to this principle that recognizes the supremacy of God. In the Judeo-Christian tradition, he said, life is seen as a gift from God, and given the sanctity attached to that gift, it is not to be brought to an end by the intentional act of another party. Decriminalizing suicide has not legitimized it.

Nelson's second ground was—more to the legal point— the public policy implications of liberalization. Assisted suicide was not solely a private act of personal freedom, he maintained. A recognized right to assisted suicide would inevitably lead to a corresponding duty to kill. The right to be killed could lead to the elderly, handicapped and chronically ill feeling they had a duty to die. Nelson concluded that the court was being asked to exercise a legislative function that was beyond its jurisdiction.

The final intervenor was People in Equal Participation Inc. (PEP), a Winnipeg-based non-profit organization for persons with severe disabilities. PEP's aim is to integrate disabled people in all aspects of community life. Providing the seriously disabled with the resources and programs necessary to live independently was part of that integration.

This group opposed Sue's application. Patrick Riley, arguing on its behalf, said that the Criminal Code Section 241(b) was consistent with Section 7 of the charter because in guaranteeing "life, liberty and security of the person" it protected those who are vulnerable and who may decide, only for a moment, that they wish death.

Riley acknowledged that there was "a differential effect" on Sue because of her physical disability, but claimed any change in the law would lead to greater discrimination.

Said Riley: "The problem is that disabled people are often not fully informed of the alternatives; that they must deal with a society which believes their lives are worthless; that financial constraints prevent the disabled from living independently; the 'death wishes' of the disabled are too readily accepted by family, physicians, courts and lawyers; and suicidal patients do not receive appropriate crisis counseling."

Sue, watching from her armchair in Saanich, found many of the arguments puzzling or amusing. What she couldn't understand was why so many people felt it their business to intrude on what she continued to regard as an issue between herself alone and the court.

One person who was not amused was John Hofsess. He was furious with Chris Considine's integration of "conditions" into Sue's application. He shortly after wrote at length about Considine's submission in *Last Rights*. His comments illustrate the enormous distance over social and legal territory that Sue had covered in her eight-month struggle. From a simple request to her friend, Hofsess, the matter had risen to the Supreme Court and in the process, its very nature had been changed.

Wrote Hofsess: "The Sue Rodriguez who came to me last August for assistance in committing suicide made it very clear that when *she* decided she had 'had enough,' no matter what others thought of her decision or condition— she wanted to be able to end her life. She felt no need to *justify* her decision to others. She had no intention of getting in the *in extremis* position of being 'near' death. She certainly did not want to suffer *unbearable* physical or *severe* psychological distress; and she did not want her decision to be second-guessed by a panel of 'experts.'"

But Sue *did* have to justify her decision. And although morphine would keep unbearable physical pain at a distance, she was to know severe psychological stress before the decision of the Supreme Court would be announced a little over four months later.

Twelve

May to September 1993

Sue Rodriguez had now joined a long line of Canadian heroes. It wasn't necessary to be a supporter of Sue's cause to admire her. There was just something about the woman —audacity, tenacity, incredible courage. And always, despite the shuffling gait of an old woman and a voice that sounded ground out of a machine whose batteries were low, there was both elegance and eloquence. For or against Sue, as the country awaited the Supreme Court decision, most people felt the way the Canadian Conference of Catholic Bishops felt—"great respect for Ms Rodriguez."

The summer of 1993 was short and moody, with a few blazing days thrown in for comfort. For Sue, the wait for the Supreme Court decision seemed interminable. The disease wasn't standing still: she could feel time running out with the passing of each day. Small things that she could do one day—such as scratch an itch on her kneecap —she could not do the next. No sooner would she adapt to losing this or that function, something else would go wrong or change. All her muscles were weakening and her whole body shifting out of alignment. Her left shoulder, completely dislocated, was now permanently held in position by foam padding, and foam pads were being positioned on other parts of her body, in order to protect her fragile skin from jutting bones.

Sue, as usual, was surrounded by a crowd of care-givers, while most central relationships in her life remained a source of pain. As Henry struggled with his business, and to be a good father to Cole and "a best friend to Sue," he could not disguise the stress he was experiencing or a growing anger at himself for having put himself in this sad situation. He felt that, instead of help-ing Sue, his presence simply added to her ongoing sense of loss.

Sue told her friend Helma Libick that Henry was "barely civil, all gloom and doom." His stress was such that, toward the end of July, he was involved in an auto accident and wiped out his car.

But then suddenly, his mood shifted. He became light-hearted, happy, and his entire attitude toward Sue changed. When he started not telling Sue where he was going or who he was going out with, she felt sure that he had met someone else. Henry admitted it was true—and it was serious. Later Sue said: "He tried desperately to be friends with me, he wanted me to approve of what he was doing. But that's a hard thing to accept, especially when I feel he had treated me badly for two years.

"Before then his mind was always someplace else. He would not look at me or really talk to me. But then, because he has a new friend and feels better about him-self, about his whole life, he wants to be friends with me. He starts talking to me and wants me to have a better relationship with him. But on his terms—with a girlfriend."

Yet Sue didn't really feel betrayed: "It's not that I thought he'd be true to me indefinitely. I just thought it was poor timing to start having an affair, simply because I feel like I'm closer to the end, closer than maybe he's aware of. But it's been two years now and I just thought, why couldn't he wait another little while?"

Said Henry: "I don't know if it was a mistake to tell Sue I'd met someone or not. I'd made the reasons why I was back in the house as clear as I could from the beginning. Sue simply wouldn't accept them. She'd tell me on one hand that she didn't care, that she wished I'd leave or she wanted to leave. But when I did meet someone, she tried to make me feel terrible. I'd been completely loyal for a year and a half under very difficult circumstances. I really wanted to be a good friend, someone she could count on —but not anything else. But I reached the point where I had to start being independent of the guilt and brain-washing she was putting on me."

Henry said that he felt Sue did not care so much about his having met someone else—as she had always known that was a possibility and had even mentioned it—but what she did care about was Henry's making his own independent decisions. "Sue wasn't used to my doing that. I'd let other people make decisions for me a lot of my life. I wanted to start making them for myself."

Sue felt that Henry saw this new relationship in terms of curing *his* disability. Henry, she said, always felt that he'd been maneuvered into doing things for other people and he'd never been able to stand up and do just what he wanted for himself. This had started in his family and had continued in his marriage. "Having a new friend and doing whatever it is he's doing, well, he thinks it's liberated him."

But for Henry, "It wasn't so much a question of being liberated. It did do that. It was a question of surviving."

Cole, now home all day on school holidays, was also feeling the stress. After going through a period of being very proud of his mother, he could barely hide his discomfort and anger at her increasing incapacity. Her inability to speak clearly or raise her voice was a constant source of grief for her and frustration for him. A polite young man, he had now taken to shouting back "What?," and if Sue repeated her suggestion, he would sometimes cry out: "I know, I'm not deaf!"

Sue realized that soon she would have to have a voice amplifier, realized more painfully that any active role as a mother would soon be over.

Had Sue been a different character she might have been able to accept these losses with some degree of resignation. But then she should not have been the fighter that she was, would not have accomplished what she did in raising the nation's consciousness about how difficult it is to die with dignity and brought to the fore society's responsibilities to ensure that this is possible.

During the summer, something happened that steeled Sue's resolve to end it before she lost all control and before her son, Cole, suffered too much. It was a very small incident but to Sue highly significant. She was in her wheelchair in the garden. Because she was no longer able to flick them off her body, Sue had developed a small phobia about bugs and spiders. Cole was pushing her wheelchair when he started to push it into a spiderweb strung between the bushes. She cried out for him to stop. To her anger at Cole and fear of spiders, was added a profound sense of helplessness, of being trapped. She cried at Cole: "No, no, stop," but he went ahead and pushed through the web, which had a big spider in the middle.

Said Sue: "It's a childlike thing; he thinks it's funny. And because of the way I react, it eggs him on to do it more. When he's away, I miss him terribly, and then he's back a couple of hours and I think what a little monster he is! I just feel so helpless. He wouldn't have gotten away with it before, but now I can't do a thing about it, just sit and see it. He's hurting terribly because he knows he's going to lose his mother, and he takes it out on me sometimes. It makes me think about what it would be like if I waited until the end, the helplessness of it all."

During this summer, a grief counselor with the Victoria Hospice Society, Eve Joseph, visited Sue on a regular basis, as did Dr. Debbie Braithwaite, who was in charge of Sue's pain management. Dr. Braithwaite and Sue talked about palliative care for Sue's final days but Sue's heart was not in it. She simply didn't want to spend that time in a narcotic coma even though the Hospice Society was willing to come into her home with 24-hour care so that she could die there without ever going into a hospital.

Sue expressed the same fears time and again whenever hospice care was mentioned. That fear was not only of a slow death but of total lack of control.

"The end would probably come about because of some sort of an infection, a mucus buildup," she said. "I'd be given morphine, increasingly over two or three days. It might take a week to die. For all that time, I'll not be coherent, not be in control. You're in their hands, and to me that would be very difficult, and terrible for my family, such a drawn-out business that's going to end in my death anyway.

"They would attach this needle to my chest where the mucus buildup would occur, and this medication would dry it up. A machine that I'd operate myself would suck mucus out of my throat. That's a very scary thing. I had a cold a year ago, I know what they are saying, and I don't want that, knowing I'm not going to live anyway."

Dr. Braithwaite simply concentrated on the task of keeping Sue as pain free and as comfortable as possible. In palliative care philosophy, mind, body and spirit live in the same place. Palliative care (palliative—"to cloak" or cover up) is based on the concept that pain is not only a matter of dealing with a sick body: other factors can contribute to and increase pain—social, financial, emotional, spiritual and even bureaucratic pain. Some of these pains can't be directly solved, but if they are recognized and articulated by the sufferer, the pain can lose its power.

According to Dr. Braithwaite, ALS is one disease that takes a great deal of pain management, not because the pain is so intense but because the progression is so variable in each patient. It's never a matter of having "the" correct dose. The disease progresses at a different rate in each person and the needs of that individual vary, as do the patient's reactions to various drugs and combinations of drugs. So it's not a matter of the doctor prescribing a formula, although a general pattern for an ALS patient is to start with Tylenol, move on to Tylenol 3 as needed, then Tylenol 3 every four hours and then morphine.

Sue's disease had progressed extremely rapidly. She was now taking Tylenol 3 with codeine, and using Fentynl (morphine) patches which are stuck to the body so that the drug is absorbed into the skin steadily. Pain is easier to prevent if it's caught before it gets started, so Dr. Braithwaite had ordered "break-through medication." When a painkiller doesn't do the job, the "break-through" dose is on hand to make sure. In chronic pain management, the solution is to be routine: medication on an "as needed" basis doesn't work. The best way is to control the pain by keeping yourself out of it.

Sue felt well cared for by Debbie Braithwaite, but despite the doctor's expertise and her warm and engaging manner, no real relationship ever developed between her and Sue. Dr. Braithwaite was a believer in palliative care to the end. Sue had a way of cutting out people whose ideas weren't in line with her own. A subtle wall dropped. Sue would accept palliative care, but only to the extent that she could control it. Beyond that, she wanted nothing of it.

Sue had said that memories of her own father's death had nothing to do with her own wish to commit suicide. Yet several times when speaking of palliative care (which her father had not had), she remarked: "I don't want my son to see me in that [my father's] state. He'll carry that vision of me for the rest of his life. That's what I remember when I think of my father." Sue was referring to her father's wasted physical appearance, and inability to speak or care for his simplest needs.

Despite her psychological and physical pain, Sue still put out great effort to enjoy life. She went regularly to the hairdresser, although that was becoming almost dangerous. A friend would drive her over to Lee Ann's Salon, in the neighborhood. She would roll down the driveway in her wheelchair, and then walk in, held up and assisted. She was determined to walk into that beauty salon for as long as she could. But it was becoming scary. Every time she went, she feared she'd fall. And her neck couldn't take it much longer. Lee Ann would build up the towels to support it, but the pain when she stretched her head back for shampooing was becoming too much. It was time to ask Lee Ann to come to the house. "It's not just a matter of a haircut," Sue said. "I have to keep the coloring up."

Her two great friends during this time were Helma and Svend. When Henry was away on weekends, Helma would come over for Saturday night.

From the time she had met Svend Robinson, he had kept in close contact with phone calls and visits. In midsummer, Svend took Sue to Vancouver for a weekend break at the Sylvia Hotel on Beach Avenue in English Bay. The memories that she had of that weekend reveal something of both Svend's character and of Sue's.

"We had a wonderful time, the two of us, in town and on the loose," she said. "Yet he's very accident-prone around me. He often forgets he has to be careful. He's so eager to get me in and out of the car, he's dropped me, and bumped me.

"One day we were in Vancouver, the same day President Clinton was in town, and we were going to take the ferry from Granville Island to Stanley Park. He went to pick me up from the wheelchair and almost broke my ribs. Another time we were going for a walk on the sea wall and stopped at a refreshment booth for hot cider. Two little girls had been separated from their father. He was apparently at home because they had him on the phone. The girls needed someone to describe to their father where they were in the park. Svend stuck the hot cider between my legs and rushed off to do his good deed on the phone. The cider splashed onto my hand and I had to sit there with this hot cider stuck between my legs and there was nothing I could do about it but take the pain.

"I teased him for months after. We had a great time but that's what I always remember when I think of that weekend. He's so impetuous and so filled with goodwill. Having to hide his homosexuality for so long has made him very sensitive to the sufferings of others."

Toward the end of July, Sue's chiropractor, Richard Elder, visited Sue at her request. Elder had treated Sue for back and neck pain since January 1989, nearly two years before she was diagnosed with ALS. Following her diagnosis, gentle minimal adjustments had given Sue temporary relief, but her condition was beyond that now.

Sue's jaw was dislocated: there were no muscles to hold it. It was hard to eat and hard to talk and despite the morphine, Sue said her jaw was painful. She had called Elder in the hope that he might be able to help. But her entire condition was beyond Elder's help; this would be his last visit.

From the onset of her illness, Sue had had one family member keep in regular touch. Her brother, Tom Shipley, who lived in Barrie, Ontario, had always considered his sister "extraordinary, the leader of the three sisters and the most outgoing and adventurous member of the family." Tom was Sue's junior by 14 months.

"Every time I saw her on television, I'd find tears on my face," he said. "But it wouldn't go any further. I didn't send her flowers or letters or anything, but about once a month I'd fax her and say something like: 'Thinking of you. Darn proud of you.' I hate phones, I hardly ever phone, and I'm too lazy to write letters. But even when I sent a fax to Sue, I hardly ever got a reply."

Tom said there was a lot of feeling and thought in his family but there was never any action. "Laziness plays a part in my family," he said. "We're also pretty inhibited. Our grandparents wanted to raise us. My grandfather would stomp on people to get what he wanted. Sue had the qualities of both my grandparents except she was very gentle and smooth at the same time."

Tom visited Sue in Saanich twice during her illness, Sally came for Christmas in 1991 and Anne came during the summer of 1992. But most of the family, said Tom, preferred not to show their feelings. "And they didn't want to be hassled or to have their names in the media. They just let Sue do her thing."

He said he knew that his mother lived close to Sue and rarely visited but he understood why. "She's very sensitive and tender, a very sweet woman. But she's had too many times of grief in her life where she couldn't do anything about it. And although I'm sure she's cried a lot about Sue, she didn't feel there was anything she could do about it. I don't want to blame everything on my grandfather and grandmother but they certainly had a long-term effect on my family."

In May 1993, Sue had a dream whose theme she later said had recurred several times in her sleep: "I was attending a party where I had dressed up with shoulder pads that were made up of feathers and pearls—quite elaborate. Someone drove me home but before we arrived he told me he liked me and would I go out with him sometime. I said yes, but didn't really want to go. And then in the next scene, he was taking me to his home where he held me prisoner for what seemed like years. While I had some freedom, any attempts to escape were unsuccessful. Other people were around who were either understanding or were being held captive as well."

Said Sue: "After the dream ended, I realized that many of my dreams involved scenarios where I am held captive and cannot escape."

"Sue could be a very charming woman, and very funny," said her neighbor, Marg Owens. "She and Henry, as a couple, were always nice to have around. Even when things were apparently not going so well between them, they were always polite to each other in public. They never made anyone else feel uncomfortable.

"I'd arranged a birthday party for her 42d. By then she was already in a wheelchair and had trouble walking. We set up tables outside in the garden, and had lots of white wine, beer and lemonade. It was a hot afternoon, lots of kids running around. The son of a neighbor, Kent Sorenson, came over and did the lawns. All her friends were there.

"Well, now her 43d was coming up and she wondered aloud to me if Henry would remember, if he was planning anything. I said to her: 'Hey, you don't expect a husband to remember birthdays. Maybe they should but they don't. You'll have to find a subtle way of reminding him.' But I don't think she did. I kept our relationship light and breezy. She tended to focus on her relationship with Henry. She expected a lot out of life."

On Sue's 43d birthday, her friend Cindy Ramsey took her out for lunch. Her friend Helma arranged a getaway for three days for Sue and her home-helper at the Hotel Bedford in downtown Victoria. Sue said they had a great time, lots of laughs. But privately she was determined this would be her last birthday. She had almost had enough of living. It was just a matter of holding on now for the decision of the Supreme Court as to whether she would suicide legally or illegally.

Dr. Sandra Elder kept in tenuous touch with Sue during this time. (Before she died, Sue asked Dr. Elder to speak to me regarding their sessions. Dr. Elder was not in the least anxious to do so, but finally agreed to at Sue's insistence. Dr. Elder is a registered grief counselor with the Association for Death Education. She has a Ph.D. from the University of Victoria in counseling psychology.) She was, perhaps, better able to understand Sue's emotional state than anyone else.

Dr. Elder said she saw Sue only occasionally after her determination to take her own life.

Said Dr. Elder: "Sue had an aching soul, and never had internal peace. She wouldn't let love in, and when you are starved for love, you sabotage any attempts people make to give it to you. There's a sort of attitude: love me, leave me alone.

"If you love, you can forgive and let go of the anger. I can say goodbye without a terrible resentment. But anger was Sue's foundation. Her identity was based on it."

Why would Sue have insisted that Dr. Elder be interviewed for her story when she must have known this portrait of her as a deeply angry woman would emerge?

"I don't know," said Dr. Elder. "All I know is that Sue wanted me to talk to you, and she must have known what I would say, because we had discussed these matters together. Perhaps she felt a total picture should come out. She was a very honest and courageous woman. She was not afraid of the truth or of reality. Perhaps she felt, as I do, that her accomplishments were of such significance that the rest paled beside it."

On September 30, 1993, the Supreme Court of Canada announced its decision. In a vote of five to four, it denied Sue's request for a physician-assisted suicide.

This last and final decision of Canada's judicial system made a parliamentary debate inevitable.

Thirteen

September 30, 1993

Those who oppose the right to die hold the traditional belief that all life is sacred, that we do not own it, God does. An estimated four out of five North Americans believe in God. And yet, if there is any validity in national polls, more than half of these people apparently support physician-assisted suicide and euthanasia at the patient's request in cases of intractable suffering and terminal illness. These views are similar to those held by secular humanists whose lives are lead outside of religious circles.

There has been a profound shift in recent years in the perception of God, and in the dignity and responsibilities of man. This is true even among religious believers who hold that life is sacred. God appears as being more merciful and compassionate, and man appears as having greater self-determination in his own fate, his own life and by logical extension, his own death.

Sue had gone to the Supreme Court of Canada with a profound belief in her right of self-determination. She perceived death and the way we die as part of life, part of her rights and part of her entitlement to human dignity under the law. She wanted to die because she was experiencing an incredible degree of psychological suffering that resulted principally from her near-paralyzed condition, and secondarily from her own particular personal situation. Sue did not want this situation exposed in her lifetime but, for whatever reason, placed no restrictions on its being revealed after her death.

The fundamental question before the court was unchanged: whether or not Criminal Code Section 241(b) forbidding assisted suicide infringed on Sue's life, liberty and security of the person as guaranteed under Section 7 of the charter.

The majority opinion, in answering that question, did so in terms that—were it not for the Charter of Rights and Freedoms—could have been written 100 years ago. The fundamental values of society were referred to time and again. The comparatively new recognition of the dignity of the person was referred to time and again. Yet there was no room allowed, or no recognition given, to the profound shifts that have taken place in social thinking on these issues within the last 25 or so years as a result of medical technology, drugs and a change in the way many people relate both to God and to society.

Whether the judgment was right or wrong, it was in its language—on what must be one of the most exciting human rights issues to come before the court—lackluster, cloudy and uninspired. It might have been clever and correct, but that did not make it persuasive. This was disappointing in view of the fact that this is an issue— unlike other issues that reach the Supreme Court—that directly affects every citizen. It was also an issue with which many citizens, either with a terminally ill family member or in their professional work, have already had to grapple. No matter where one stands on the issue, the Supreme Court judgment was in marked contrast to the precision, clarity and force of Chief Justice Allan McEachern's judgment at the appeal court level. That judgment made Justice McEachern's stand, and the legal reasons for it, crystal clear to every citizen who was literate.

The Supreme Court majority opinion was written by Mr. Justice John Sopinka, a well-known trial lawyer, a barrister of great experience and, according to one who knows him, "down to earth, unpretentious and very smart." Obviously, he decided to give a strict legal interpretation and leave any trace of the human rights drama inherent in the issue to Parliament to decide. His opinion was agreed to by Justices Gérard La Forest, Charles Gonthier, Frank Iacobucci and John Major. These five justices found that Section 241(b) did indeed infringe on Sue's rights under Section 7 but not to the extent that this violation would offend against the principles of fundamental justice. It was therefore allowable and Sue's case was dismissed.

"The expression 'principles of fundamental justice' in Section 7 implies that there is some consensus that these principles are vital or fundamental to our societal notion of justice," said Justice Sopinka. "They must be capable of being identified with some precision . . . and they must also be legal principles." That is, these principles can't be so broad that they are vague generalizations about what our society considers to be ethically acceptable, and these principles must also be part of the basic tenets of our legal system.

"Fundamental justice requires that a fair balance be

struck between the interests of the state and those of the individual. The respect for human dignity, while one of the underlying principles upon which our society is based, is not a principle of fundamental justice within the meaning of Section 7."

Justice Sopinka then referred to the long-standing blanket prohibition on assisted suicide as "grounded in the state interest in protecting life, and [it reflected] the policy of the state that human life should not be depreciated by allowing life to be taken. This blanket prohibition was the norm among Western democracies and had never been adjudged to be unconstitutional or contrary to fundamental human rights.

"No consensus can be found in favor of the decriminalization of assisted suicide," said Justice Sopinka. "To the extent there is a consensus, it is that human life must be respected. This consensus finds legal expression in our legal system which prohibits capital punishment. The prohibition against assisted suicide serves a similar purpose.

"Sanctity of life . . . has been understood historically as excluding freedom of choice in the self-infliction of death and certainly in the involvement of others in carrying out that choice. At the very least, no new consensus has emerged in society opposing the right of the state to regulate the involvement of others in exercising power over individuals ending their lives."

Justice Sopinka spoke of the protection of the vulnerable who might be induced in moments of weakness to suicide, the history of suicide provisions and finally—a point of considerable significance—his judgment recognized the distinction based on intent—the so-called "double effect."

Glanville Williams, an English jurist whose book, *The Sanctity of Life and the Criminal Law* is considered a classic in the area of euthanasia and assisted suicide, describes this principle as follows: "Where a patient is suffering from an incurable and agonizing disease, and ordinary quantities of a drug fail to render the pain tolerable, many doctors will give the minimum dose necessary to kill the pain, knowing that this dose at the same time is an amount likely to kill the patient. In other words, faced with the choice of either doing nothing, or killing both the pain and the patient, the doctor chooses the latter course. Catholics accept this on their principle of double effect. The will of the doctor is directed to the relief of suffering, an effect which he achieves. It is merely a secondary effect that the patient is killed."

Williams then speaks of the "artificiality" of this distinction: the doctor giving the overdose is not guilty of wrongdoing provided he keeps his mind steadily off the consequences which his professional training teaches him is inevitable—that is, the death of the patient.

However, Williams backtracks on the charge of artificiality by concluding: "When you know that your conduct will have two consequences, one in itself good and one in itself evil, you are compelled as a moral agent to choose between acting and not acting by making a judgment of value, that is to say that the good is to be more desired than the evil is to be avoided. If this is what the principle of double effect means, well and good."

As overdosing to kill intractable pain in the terminally

ill who are close to death is not rare in Canada, it was significant that the Supreme Court clarified the legality of this practice.

Clearly, the stand of the majority in the Rodriguez decision was based on the notion of the Supreme Court as being a protector of the consensus of public opinion and a defender of values that society holds dear.

Yet, the majority opinion was a majority of only one vote. There were three dissenting opinions for a total of four dissenting votes.

The chief justice, Antonio Lamer, wrote one of the dissenting opinions.

Chief Justice Lamer did not consider Sections 7 and 12 because he found that Criminal Code Section 241(b) infringed on Section 15 of the charter.

"In my view, persons with disabilities who are or will become unable to end their lives without assistance are discriminated against by that provision since, unlike persons capable of causing their own deaths, they are deprived of the option of choosing suicide," the chief justice said.

Individuals in Canadian society are not only protected against direct, deliberate discrimination, but also against incidental or indirect discrimination. An apparently neutral rule, one that applies to all equally, may also have the effect of discriminating against a disadvantaged group. This is indirect discrimination and the courts have held in a number of cases that this is also covered by the charter.

"Even in imposing generally applicable provisions, the government must take into account differences which in fact exist between individuals and so far as possible ensure that the provisions adopted will not have a greater impact on certain classes of persons due to irrelevant personal characteristics, than on the public as a whole," said Justice Lamer.

Section 241(b) created an inequality because it prevents persons physically unable to end their lives unassisted from choosing suicide when that option is open to others. The basis of this inequality was physical disability, a ground of discrimination under Section 15. Even though it was not Parliament's intent to discriminate and even though Section 241(b) does not single out the disabled, it has the *effect* of discriminating.

"Can it be said that the intent of Parliament in retaining Section 241(b), after repealing the offense of attempted suicide, was to acknowledge the primacy of self-determination for physically able people alone?"

Justice Lamer believed not. He therefore ordered a constitutional exemption for those who are physically unable to commit suicide unassisted, to be granted on terms laid out by Chief Justice McEachern of the B.C. Court of Appeal. He would, however, eliminate the court order granting the exemption, which Justice McEachern required, and he saw no reason not to extend the permission to a terminally ill patient to have another person assist in ending their life—as Sue had requested.

Madame Justice Beverley McLachlin, with Madame Claire L'Heureux-Dubé agreeing, believed the entire case was about Section 7 of the charter, that is, about making decisions about one's own body. Justice McLachlin held that Section 241(b) infringed on Section 7 of the charter through the notions of dignity and the right to privacy, and also held that this infringement (contrary to Justice Sopinka) was not in accord with fundamental justice.

"In my view, the denial to Sue Rodriguez of a choice available to others cannot be justified. The potential for abuse is amply guarded against by existing provisions in the Criminal Code. I cannot agree that the failure of Parliament to address the problem of the terminally ill is determinative of this appeal. Nor do I agree that the fact that medically assisted suicide has not been widely accepted elsewhere bars Sue Rodriguez's claim. Since the advent of the charter, this court has been called upon to decide many issues which formerly lay fallow. If a law offends the charter, this court has no choice but to so declare."

And Criminal Code Section 241(b) did violate the charter, in Madame Justice McLachlin's judgment, by limiting the right to deal with one's own body.

"What is the difference between suicide and assisted suicide that justifies making one lawful and the other a crime, that justifies allowing some this choice, while denying it to others?

"It is argued that the denial to Sue Rodriguez of the capacity to treat her body in a way available to the physically able is justified because to permit assisted suicide will open the doors, if not the floodgates, to the killing of disabled persons who may not truly consent to death. The argument is essentially this: there may be no reason on the facts of Sue Rodriguez's case for denying to her the choice to end her life, a choice that the physically able have available to them. But she must be denied that choice because of the danger that other people may wrongfully abuse the power over the weak and ill, and may end the lives of these persons against their consent. Thus, Sue Rodriguez is asked to bear the burden of the chance that other people in other situations may act criminally to kill others or improperly sway them to suicide. She is asked to serve as a scapegoat."

Preventing Sue from exercising autonomy over her own body for the reasons (cited above) offends against fundamental justice. Justice McLachlin therefore agreed to the remedy set out by Chief Justice Antonio Lamer.

Mr. Justice Peter de Carteret Cory's judgment was brief. In essence, he stated that life includes dying, that dying is an integral part of living, and is therefore protected under Section 2. The right to die is as protected as any other aspect of the right to life.

"State prohibitions that would force a dreadful, painful death on a rational but incapacitated terminally ill patient are an affront to human dignity," he said.

He said he saw no difference between permitting a person of sound mind to refuse treatment and permitting a person of sound mind to choose death with dignity by having another terminate life-preserving treatment. He also saw no reason not to extend the permission to a terminally ill patient to have another person assist in ending that patient's life, as requested by Sue. He supported the judgment of Chief Justice Lamer and would use the same conditions to deal with the matter.

Our society is becoming increasingly concerned over the life and death issues surrounding "death with dignity."

While the varying judgments of the Supreme Court were in agreement on some critical points—for example, that Section 241(b) infringed on Sue's rights in Section 7 of the charter—there was no consensus as to the degree of offense caused by this infringement.

It's fair to say that neither the majority or minority opinions, ranging widely and having little consensus, and concerned naturally with legal niceties, have helped to clarify the thinking of ordinary citizens who are deeply concerned with these issues.

These concerns are, as is obvious, affected by the law, but they are seen primarily as very human issues, not legal issues. They range from a fear of being "put down" by a physician who is a stranger to you and who believes your life is not worth living, to the fear of being hooked onto a machine, or sustained on some drug or by other technological means and being kept alive against your wishes.

In between these extremes is a whole range of attitudes and concerns, including those where family relationships are such that there is no confidence that one's demise won't be arranged. There are other situations where a person might want to let go, but is deeply concerned that if this is arranged with a relative, that relative might be plagued by guilt for the rest of his or her days. Even a physician who has assisted may later deeply regret it—or may later regret refusing to assist. And of recent years we have seen case after case where lengthy public court battles—Nancy B. v. Hotel-Dieu de Quebec, Nancy Cruzan v. Director, Missouri Department of Health—have added grievously to the terrible sufferings of the victims' families.

What is right in a secular, pluralistic society? Outside of religious circles, the right to die isn't considered a serious philosophical problem. Secular humanists have always held that terminally ill people have the right to die. Our ability to be rational and exercise free will is—not only in the humanist tradition but also in traditional religion—what separates us from animals. Secular humanists believe that when these faculties are going to be inevitably lost, suicide can be a rational and courageous act.

However, if one believes that human life is absolutely sacred, and that God, not us, owns it, the position of the secular humanists is intolerable. Yet society "plays God" in other areas. Extraordinary means are used to prolong life way beyond what is "natural," it is acceptable to kill other human beings, even innocent beings, in war. In the United States, people are "legally" killed by the state justice systems. Where does the killing of a terminally ill person in intractable pain who is mentally competent and asks for help, fit into all this? It is only in recent years that millions of people are living beyond their seventies. Perhaps it might be as "natural" to want to die when one is in one's eighties or nineties as it is to want to live when one is young. Is it possible that modern medicine can keep the body alive beyond the limit of the spirit? Certainly it is: any nurse in an old person's home is familiar with this.

Most people agree with the right to die with dignity, but what does dignity mean? People's idea of dignity varies greatly, as we can see from the solemnity that surrounds the deathbed of a prime minister in Canada to the wailing and shrieking deemed suitable for a Middle Eastern potentate.

Sue Rodriguez had her own clear concept of dying with dignity and was willing to fight the Supreme Court of Canada to affirm it. Mr. Justice Sam Filer of the Ontario Court, general division, who has ALS, has his own clear concept of dignity. He has successfully fought the Judicial Council which tried to have him removed from the bench "due to infirmity," to quote the language of the Judges Act. Mae Dang, who died in January 1993, at 53, was a wife and the mother of two sons. She lived with ALS for 16 years and died with dignity—yet she supported Sue's "right" to assisted suicide. Stephen Hawking, who has lived with a type of ALS for 30 years, said he would never take his own life—but he believed Sue Rodriguez had the right to do so.

Toni Eareckson Tada, in her book *When Is It Right To Die* quotes James 1:5: "If any of you does not know how to meet a particular problem, he has only to ask God and he may be quite sure that the necessary wisdom will be given him."

When told of this, Sue replied: "I have listened very deeply to my interior spirit and believe this is the right thing for me to do. That was the wisdom given to me."

So with the Supreme Court decision in, Sue Rodriguez was back to square one. She would, by her own lights, be "forced" to commit an illegal act. Because Supreme Court, or not, she had made up her mind.

Fourteen

November to December 1993

Now that the legal struggle is over, Sue's energy is draining from her body as if her skin were cheesecloth. She had always known she might lose, but hope for a victory had kept her going, had given her motivation and the possible solution to her desire to die. A win would have been a public recognition of her value, an affirmation of her significance.

She bears the rejection well, speaks publicly and eloquently of her disappointment, but gives no indication that it's a shard in the heart, a final rejection in a long line of rejections. Her sense of abandonment is profound. The home-helpers feel it in the sudden weightiness of her skeletal body. It is as if a framework within her tall, gaunt, now-angular body has been dismantled. In the mornings the change is particularly noticeable. Her limbs are locked tight, she is reluctant to leave the comfort of the high-tech hospital-style bed and her proud spirit seems heavy with the sense of failure.

For months now, her bed has been made up with satin sheets to comfort and protect the limbs that, deprived of sun, are marble white. Weeks earlier, her coccyx broke through her taut skin, but the small wound, aggravated by 24 hours of bearing her weight, is still sore and bloody and will never heal, despite the cream and the gauze dressings. Now in the mornings, she longs to lie there, dreading the separation from the comfort of the sheets, the drabness of the day ahead, the exhausting effort of simply living. It is not as if there is somebody waiting to embrace her, to say with love and sincerity how happy they are she is still with them, to hear with genuine interest how she spent the night, whether she slept or dreamed. Awakening to the day, she awakes to loneliness.

In the morning when Nadine arrives, the increasingly breathless struggle to get through another monotonous day begins. Nadine gently lifts Sue's limbs one by one, barely flexes them, gently rotates them, coaxing them back into a reluctant life. This done, Nadine moves Sue to the edge of the bed, swings Sue's legs over and helps her sit up. She then dresses her and fixes a thick white transfer belt around Sue's waist. Facing her, Nadine helps Sue to her feet, her right arm around Sue's waist holding on to the belt, her left arm out for Sue to use as a sort of handle, to steady her balance.

But it really isn't a matter of steadying her balance anymore. Now Sue and Nadine sometimes stand there perfectly still, one, two minutes, making certain Sue has the strength just to take the first step. Nadine sees the struggle in Sue's grave, green eyes as the seconds pass, sees the occasional twitch of her mouth, hears the still rarer cry: "Oh, Nadine! I just can't get my legs to move anymore!" But soon, slowly, she does move one foot forward, and lockstepped, Nadine now behind her, they shuffle as if doing a macabre dance to the bathroom, then to the glide chair at the foot of the stairs.

Nadine is deeply torn. If she informs the home care

agency of Sue's trouble walking, the home-makers will be forbidden to help her walk, ordered to keep her in a wheelchair at all times. Nadine knows that would be setting the date of Sue's death.

Sue, stubborn and iron-willed once she is finally moving, unaware of the fears of her home-helpers, insists on walking wherever possible in the house. She is terrified of a fall, but more terrified of sentencing her proud, mountain-climbing legs to death by wheelchair.

And so the days go by, full of dangerous and awkward little chores, morphine-induced sleepiness when the dosage is changed and unending sadness. Everyone around Sue feels the changes in her body and spirit by the way she leans on them, pressing her weight against an arm intended simply as a check to balance.

Her body has almost completely betrayed her. Both shoulders are now permanently dislocated; her neck has become a column hot with interior irritation at its own inability to find some position of comfort. She can still chew and swallow small quantities of solids, but her body, sluggish with morphine, only partially works. She is off both morphine patches and liquid morphine, but is taking 150 milligrams in pill form every day. Every other day a nurse comes in to give her an enema. She knows she is nearing the end, not necessarily of life, but of a life that she can identify as worth living.

The hope that keeps her going now is that someone will write a book that records these last years of her life and her struggle, both public and private, to die with dignity. She has asked me to write it.

On this day she tells me she's glad I've come, that she can't go on much longer. "I feel," she says, trailing off. I can't understand what she feels and lean forward; she tries again. "Crumpled. I feel I'm crumpling up like a piece of tin pressure from both ends."

She tilts her chin slightly up and, with effort, swallows. Physically, she is a stranger compared to the woman I met at a press conference 14 months earlier. She talks of cramps: they are now worse in the evenings. She is so stiff, someone must forcibly bend her legs to move them. The struggle to keep going is terrible. Just to keep clean is exhausting.

I've seen part of the struggle—Sue lowered into the bath on a levered platform, raised out, toweled down, her teeth brushed by others, her hair combed by others, the sleepy, drugged-out day that follows when the morphine dose is raised until her body adjusts to it. All of it just to keep going.

"It's so boring, so mundane, day after day, hour after hour, the same routine month after month," she says. She is not looking for pity. She is asking without asking: do you *really* understand what it's like to live in a body that is already dead? It's clear that she's had enough, that in the face of her grief she has made a decision. It's not hard to guess what. From that moment in April 1992, when she realized there was no cure and no escape from an early death, she has let anyone who would listen know that quality of life is everything to her, quantity without quality is nothing. And for Sue, there can be no quality without control. This is not a preference but a psychological need transformed into a value. When all joy in living has gone and only an existence remains, it is time to leave. She feels no duty to anyone to suffer to the end.

She is not surprised that her determination to die by her own hand is unshaken. She has no regrets about having fought to a point where she must rely on someone else to order her own death. She has loved the fight. The word she finds herself using time and again is *incredible*. Just thinking of it satisfies her enormously. She smiles happily when recounting the way people recognize her on the streets of Victoria and Vancouver. "When I started, I never imagined it would be like this," she says, and sighs deeply, slowly, with sheer satisfaction.

Svend phones her regularly, and no more than three weeks ever go by without him coming out to Cromarty Avenue and spending time with her. She tells him she wants to die before Christmas, that there is no point in living. Svend doesn't agree; he persuades her to hold on, tells her that there is yet more life to be lived. If it weren't for Cole, already anticipating Christmas, she would wonder what it is.

She has now, in her own mind, no alternative but to break the law in order to die with dignity—although she is confident that one day her cause will win. Yet she is sensitive to the ramifications of breaking the law with an assisted suicide. She speaks of sleeping capsules and liquid morphine, the deadly combination prescribed in *Final Exit*, and it is what Sue will finally use with the help of the mysterious physician.

"I'd feel so much better taking my life legally, instead of stashing sleeping pills around and risking a mishap. I don't want my son thinking I'd go behind the law—how can he ever respect it if I don't follow it? I really didn't want my last act tainted with illegality."

From these words it is clear that Sue has already decided on the method of committing suicide.

One wet day with the fog coming in great drifts from the Pacific Ocean, she sits in her office and talks with Dr. Donald Lovely about "the future." He is deeply moved by Sue's plight, but he cannot become involved in any illegal act. He suggests home hospice care. Sue is astounded to see that there are tears in his eyes. Those tears are as precious as diamonds to her. She holds them in her heart; it is empty of practically all other consolation. She has not spoken to her mother for weeks; Henry and she talk but the desperate longing to be friends is still being played out against an increasingly uneven playing field. So the tears of Dr. Lovely fall into her sore heart like balm. She tells me the next day that if there is a God, then he or she must be made of compassion.

Her gratitude to Dr. Lovely is not enough to be swayed by his advice. She refuses to die at home under a combination of care from him and hospice, or Dr. Braithwaite and hospice. The slowness of the hospice dying procedure infuriates her. Why give morphine over four, five or seven days to slow down the heart when death is inevitable anyway? Who gains by such suffering?

"If I were in that situation, I'd go away to a hospice so Cole's home wouldn't be turned into a death ward," she says. "That would be my last gesture of love to him—to give up my home and go into hospice."

She is talking rhetorically. She has found someone to help her die. Now it is just a matter now of setting the date.

Fifteen

Sue sits in the small office, waiting, her figure bolt upright and stiff in the costly wheelchair. There is foam cushioning at her back, under her buttocks and on the left armrest of her chair. She is wearing stirrup pants with heavy socks to the knees; her legs are as thin as sticks. When I enter, her head turns slightly and slowly toward the door: "Hi, how are you?" The voice is generally without pitch or tone, yet she manages a slight emphasis on the "you." The words are all joined. Her green eyes smile a welcome but the facial muscles barely move. This interview will be difficult for both of us: for her to speak, for me to understand.

Nadine has just washed Sue's hair. Brushed back, it clings smooth and wet to her head. For the first time, its true color is showing along the scalp, a line of dull gray. She will tell anyone who asks how it went gray in her late twenties, how she has dyed it since, what fun she'd had experimenting. She is not a woman to think dying hair is something to be shy about. When Cole was small, Sue dyed it honey-blond and wore it curly and shoulder-length before finally going back to the titian that went so well with her eyes.

I draw up a chair and sit directly before her. The foot-rest of the $12,000 wheelchair is slightly extended. I'm not close enough to catch her weak voice so I move in to the side, squeezed between the desk and the cold steel of the chair's wheels. It's a small office, compact with well-organized cabinets, a phone with an answering machine, a cellular phone and a fax machine sitting on the desk. Through the wall-length window there's a view of the path and garden: anyone arriving or leaving can be seen from it.

For a while we simply sit looking at each other. Everything is worn thin, her voice, face, legs. I put my hand over hers. I feel birdlike bones, the tissue-thin covering of tight skin, the cold of her fingertips unchanged by the warmth of mine. She is exhausted and dying, although a natural death could be many months away. I say anxiously: "You shouldn't let your hair stay wet like that, you'll catch your death of cold," and we both start to giggle like ten-year-olds.

But Sue's mirth is hollow, a matter of tension. She is more depressed now than she has ever been. She remarks on this: "I have been happy until now." Astonishingly, for all her grief and anger, this is by and large true. Her capacity to enjoy life has been extraordinary, shuffling on legs as spindly as stilts, sitting on a bum no bigger than a doughnut, weak lungs pulling in air to exhale in gasps of laughter, her sense of the ridiculous finding unlimited material in her own decline. Sue's friend Sharon Bartlett once told of Sue's reactions when she was given an "aid"— a helmet with a light attached to it, such as miners wear, the light to be used to point to objects when Sue could no longer speak. Sue had put it on: she and Sharon became hysterical with laughter.

And despite the effort involved, her standards of social etiquette have remained high: her table is always well set, her meals carefully and exquisitely prepared; she never failed to order flowers for anyone who had done her a favor.

She is saying now that she feels good about her life. "I've lived it to the full," she says. "Even though I've been living a tragedy, I've felt a sense of freedom. I have gained and learned from suffering. I want you to record this because it's what's happened to me. I really do accept my illness now. I accept it with love and deep appreciation. Mine is not a terrible fate for I feel I've accomplished something I never dreamed was possible."

Sue's words do not ring quite true. Neither the language nor the sentiments are Sue's usual style. A small part of me wonders if she has perhaps read them somewhere, and has, with all her heart, willed these sentiments to be her own—which they then indeed would be.

As she speaks, her eyelids droop, languorously open and close for one, two minutes. A few hours ago, Sue's morphine dose was increased: it will take a day before her body adjusts. The wave of sleepiness passes and she resumes:

"I'm not enjoying life as much. Emotionally, psychologically, things are becoming more depressing. Henry does stupid, shitty things because he is so confused and doesn't know how to behave. I tell him I care for him in the hope he will snap out of this inexcusable behavior. But he says the only way he can get through all this is to have this relationship with his new girlfriend. He has made it official in that he says he will stay with her three days a week." (I learned later that Henry never followed through.)

Her hurt is so bulky it fills the room.

I imagine Cole with his luminous eyes and nine-year-old's heart absorbing this tragic tangle of adult lives, listening to the talk of suicide and love and death and processing it all. Sue said she'd suggested Cole meet the girlfriend. "I thought it best. I thought Cole might be upset with Henry away so much. I asked Henry if he'd told Cole what it would be like once I've gone. I felt angry and worried: 'Tell him you have a girlfriend,' I said. So Henry did. Cole said: 'So, what's she like? Does she have any kids?'"

Sue swallows with effort.

"Last night Helma came over. I dictated a letter to Cole and we made a tape of it. I said I was sorry that I would not be here to watch him grow up. I said there were things I wanted to continue to teach him. More than anything, I asked him to have respect, understanding and compassion for other human beings. Be patient with your father, I said, being a single parent is not easy and things will not always be easy for him. I told him how special I thought he was and pointed out some of his good qualities. But I also let him know how important it was to learn right from wrong."

A long pause. Sue's mouth is dry, the skin of her face, drawn tight, is creamy and unblemished. Her lids again close. Finally: "I tried to help him understand why I was going to take my life. I finished my letter this way: 'I have decided to leave now because my body is deteriorating and I don't want to suffer anymore, nor do I want you to have to watch me.'"

Sue then said that she was very close to losing all voice. This is her great fear: loss of her voice will take with it all control over decisions regarding her life and her death. "You're in their hands [the medical profession], and to me that would be terrible, and such a drawn-out business for my family—only to end in my death anyway." Every time palliative care had been mentioned, she'd voiced the same fear. She saw no dichotomy between her distrust of physicians and her support of physician-assisted suicide.

"There are times during the day now when I simply cannot speak. In the mornings I usually can, but by the afternoon I can't. I have a machine downstairs that will communicate for me. It has phrases built into it and a device that will activate it. But I am losing movement so quickly. Besides, I don't know how to use it." Her eyes light up and she half smiles: "Because I've no intention of ever using it."

"You've found someone who will kill you," I say. Yes, she says, she's found a doctor who would do it "on principle." "I am telling you because you are writing the book and I want it to be complete. Somebody has to take the plunge."

Sue then says she has decided on a date. She will not say when. I don't want to know when. She will not say who. I thought, this is a woman who, for all her national fame, has no long-term, intimate sustaining love in her life except that of a mother for her own son. In fact, she has no close relationships with anyone except a couple of very recent friends keenly interested in physician-assisted suicide. I think of Dr. Elder's words: "Sue wouldn't let love in. When you are starved for love, you sabotage it."

I had to ask her, knowing the cruelty of it: "Would this have happened at this time—would it have happened at all—if you and Henry had found a way to be the best friends you sought to be?"

"Not only that," she says, meaning, not only Henry has caused her pain. She recounts two incidents which she cannot brush aside: they've sunk into her shredded heart like dye into absorbent cloth. She, too, causes herself pain. Everything hurts disproportionately: she is bruised body and soul.

These incidents serve as further "proof" that it is time to go. Doe had called Henry to see if his family was all right following the Los Angeles earthquake. Henry assured her they were, and then asked if she'd like to speak to Sue, who was sitting beside him. Mother and daughter had not spoken for a couple of weeks. Doe said, "No, just give her my love."

Doe, who is 70, maybe doesn't hear too well, I suggest. I don't say I, too, have difficulty understanding Sue sometimes. But Sue says no. She does not believe there is anything wrong with Doe's hearing. Her certainty in this respect has been polished by other remembered resentments. She does believe her mother "is a real mystery." (Doe later says she could not understand a word Sue said on the phone, that it was painful to try to understand. Then she added that there wasn't really any point anyway in just saying hello.)

Sue, her words slurring with fatigue, now tells of a friend who has an empty house in Victoria and she, Sue, wanted to go there for a few days' break. "She was so enthusiastic about my going there and then she never mentioned it again. So I didn't raise it. I wish she'd spoken to me directly. She discussed it with others, but not with me."

She is very weak. Tears spill down her cheeks. There is probably nothing sadder on earth than a dying person weeping. Then the words rattle out one by one, memorial stones to a lost life. "I don't count like other people anymore. I'm a crumpling person."

"Crumpling," I repeat. I kneel beside her and kiss her cheek. After a while I say, "Crumpling . . . it's a lovely word." We catch each other's eye and start, insanely, to laugh. "It's all nerves," I say, "the reason we are laughing."

"Oh, it can't be," she says. "All my nerves are dead."

We go off into a fit of stifled laughter. When we stop, I hurry off, happy she has laughed, amazed at the complexity of her multilayered personality, and thinking I will never see her again.

Tuesday, February 8 1994

I pick up the phone during the week and hear the slow unintelligible drawl and, gradually, listening intently, realize it's Sue asking me to come back. At the familiar sound, I feel a sense of reprieve.

When I walk in to the little office, it's clear that she has thought a great deal about our last meeting and now, only days before her death, wants to ensure her message is understood. She knows, although we've not discussed it specifically, that generally I believe that people—unless they are in unbearable pain—stay if they are loved and wanted, go if they are unloved and unwanted.

"Society assumes in a normal death of a family

member that people are surrounding them and showing their love and support," she says, swallowing hard. She's prepared a little speech. Her hair, as usual, is clean and glossy. She has a huge collection of beautiful drop earrings, mostly in silver and semiprecious stones, and the long silver and green tourmaline pendants she is wearing today are stylish and tasteful. She has put on a little lipstick and wears a forest green top and skirt. Gigi would have approved.

"I know there is nothing I can do about it. Whether I die tomorrow or wait two years, there is nothing I can do to change my basic situation." Her voice is very firm. "It is an unfortunate situation but it is not the only reason that I am ready to go. As I told you, everything is so boring, so repetitious, day after day, month after month.

"I feel for my family, for my mother, for Henry, for my son. I feel it has been going on for too long. Even the home-makers I have, I can sense it in the way in which people touch me. Maybe there should be an endless supply of people with patience and commitment. But there isn't. That's the reality. I wish people, like the courts, would deal with these things and forget their theories.

"Everything has to be done for me and it's getting worse. Even at night, sitting watching television, I have trouble resting my head. It's getting harder to hold it up because all my muscles are going, but even when I lie down, I can't get comfortable. If I need a drink, my home-maker brings a cup in a special container, but I can't hold on to the container anymore.

"I'm not in pain. Dr. Braithwaite's responsible for controlling that, but I'm in discomfort most of the time and it's getting harder to communicate. I'm at my best right now [it was 11 a.m.] but it's taking a lot of energy to project my voice. Nobody's around me long enough to see what hurdles I have to get through just to survive a day. I respect the courts and their decision but I feel it would have been nice if they could have spent a week here with me observing the realities. When you have all these physical things happening to you, and they are progressive, you just look forward to moving on."

I say that I can understand that. At this, against her will, she again weeps. She is weakened by illness and heartbreak: it's hard to say which is the more devastating. She has wanted me there to make absolutely sure my heart is open to the horror she is experiencing and to respect her resolution to end it. Her crying is terrible, out of her depths, out of someplace where I've never been.

It is her son whom she cannot leave but feels she must. He had come home from school with a report that needed a signature, and she had wanted to sign it. Her writing is now the large uncontrolled scrawl of a first-grader. He had taken it from her and run off. She said he spends most of his quality time with the home-maker. It is simply time for her to move out of his life.

She asks me to get a Kleenex and wipe her eyes. Her turned-up nose is red and tears are pooled in the deep cavities where her neck joins the collarbone. "I am in so much pain," she says. "If I were not dying I would overcome it, would pick myself up and go on living. But this is too much. It is time to leave. There's no reason to stay."

I listen in silence. Any words I might say would be just

sounds without meaning. Any meaning I might have would be for me, not for her. Any truths I would draw on would be my truths, not hers. What could I say that would not be cruel in the face of her reality?

I am not here for an exchange of views, but to enter into her world and bring back what understanding and wisdom I can from it. So we sit facing each other, silent, waiting for the wave of grief to recede. When it does, she is her old self.

"So," I say, "you've decided to take off and leave us to our own devices on our sad old planet Earth. Are you going to tell me about it?"

She smiled. No, not the exact day, just the fact it's been decided on. I ask if it's February 26, the anniversary of her father's death, and at that she says dryly: "I'm not as melodramatic as that!"

I ask how it's come about, and she tells a story of a couple of people having been in the picture, but they'd changed their minds because of the publicity. This person, she says, had been unsure, but quite recently he'd indicated he would help. I press for details. Would he come through the front door, or go around the back, and enter across the flagstone patio and through the sliding door of her downstairs bedroom? Is there not a danger the home-maker will recognize him?

No, says Sue, it will not be like that.

So, I say, the home-maker will be sent out on a message? Could she not return while the doctor was still there?

Again Sue says no: "There will be no home-maker on

that night at all, because it will take several hours to kill me."

"So morphine will be used in increasing doses, enough to finally stop the heart?"

She says yes. I say that morphine often doesn't kill, even in massive doses, it must be mixed with something else. She says that is true. We are talking as if exchanging recipes. I cannot believe this conversation: it is all hideous.

"The front door will be unlocked," she calmly continues, having decided to ignore my discomfort. She is enjoying describing her death: fairly or unfairly, I sense in Sue an anger that is both deep and pleasurable, an anger at the way things are and a pleasure at outwitting those institutions that would contain her. And perhaps in all fairness there is deep pleasure in anticipation of an end to suffering which I can't imagine. "I will be here alone on my bed downstairs, helped there by the home-maker and apparently ready for rest. I can't say where Henry and Cole will be as I have to protect everyone, but neither of them will be here."

What of the innocent party who will find her body in the morning? Or will a notice be left on her door directing the reader to call the coroner's office? She says there'd be no shock, no such thing would happen. Her plans are carefully laid.

Sue then says that her only disappointment is that she senses intuitively I do not support what she is doing. I say we all have to live by our own lights: my lights are not hers. I have not had the experience of living in protracted misery: if I ever do, perhaps her knowledge will become mine. Is there no way of speaking about these things that doesn't sound a bit pompous?

I can hear how my words sound, and how cruel my next question, yet I feel compelled to ask her again: "And you, if you were surrounded by love, by a family that hugged and kissed you and brought hot soup, and a husband who held you precious, brought you flowers, rubbed your back. Sweet Suzie, would you now be doing this?"

She replies with her usual honesty and integrity: "I don't know. I don't know." Each word was emphatic: I . . . don't . . . know. She can hardly breathe for grief. When she recovers, we sit together, my arm around her shoulder, this time her cold fingers over mine. I say for her: "But that isn't your reality." She says: "No, not my reality."

I leave early to return to Vancouver. The sea is choppy and as the ferry enters Active Pass, snow begins to fall. By the time we reach the Vancouver side, the light flakes are a soft two inches deep, covering winter's shabby brown with a fresh and false white coat. Driving home, scarcely able to see through the sleet, I weep.

Sixteen

February 11, 1994

Three years have passed since Sue Rodriguez felt the first stirrings of the disease that has consumed her life, two and a half years since physicians named it and removed all hope. These years which have turned her body into a rigid block have infused her will with iron. Her heart is another matter. It remains the heart of a mother. It has built no immunity, no resistance to pain. No dosage of morphine can help it. The thought of leaving Cole would drown her if the heart could weep.

The long-arranged meeting with someone who, at her behest, will help her to kill herself, is only hours away. She feels at peace. The pains and stresses of the past two years are already receding. Her legal struggle for physician-assisted suicide has been the first battle in the war for euthanasia in Canada and she is deeply satisfied that she has led it. She has made the whole country aware of the existence of ALS, the fate of those afflicted by it and the pressing need for well-funded research. More than anything, she has made the whole country aware of how difficult it is to die with dignity, and the responsibility of society to ensure that services are in place so that people can.

She believes that she has played the role she was meant to play and has become who she was meant to be. She is calm and single-minded on this day, the last full day of her life.

Tomorrow, she will breakfast with her family then go to her office. When Henry and Cole leave, it is from there that she will bid them goodbye. Soon after, at about 10 a.m., Svend will arrive. An hour later, the doctor will enter through the back door. She will meet with the doctor in the kitchen. Svend will then help her downstairs in the glide chair and carry her into bed. She anticipates the end of her sufferings with deep satisfaction.

Her mind is marvelously clear, as if it had gained in acuity the strengths her body now lacks. She sees her suicide as a solution that is efficient and practical. She refuses to allow into her consciousness those who might question or oppose her. She is indifferent to beliefs that there are deeper truths beyond the appearance of things and that these must be explored and encountered in the process of becoming fully human. She is convinced because of the attention paid to her by the media that the taking of her own life is acceptable to society. She is innocently unaware of its entertainment value.

Her will has not weakened because the highest court in the land has denied legitimacy to her beliefs. She is certain her voice will be heard in the end. She is deeply imbued with the belief that people have not only the right but the responsibility to determine the shape of their own lives. She has logically extended this belief to include the shape of her own death.

This shaping of a life out of nothing but her own experiences and integrity has not made Sue a saint. The disease that is killing her, that has enabled her on one level to be consistently courageous, honorable and strong, has not brought any solution to the problems of her private and personal life. Though she is funny, charming and sweet socially, Sue's anger remains her foundation. She will take the cause of this anger, whose roots trail back into childhood, unexamined and unresolved with her to the grave. She struggles to overcome resentment toward her mother: the will to forgive is there but so is the power of anger.

Toward Henry she makes no such effort: her attachment to this anger is deep. She nurtures it with sullen words and sharp rejections to his overtures of friendship. She knows the ambivalence of his support springs from a genuine agony but she cannot relinquish her rage despite its hairbreadth distance from overwhelming need and grief.

Revealingly, in her financial affairs she has made arrangements to maintain control even after her death. She has kept secret from Henry the fact that, shortly after he moved back home following her diagnosis, she saw her lawyer and changed the "title in common" to their home to "tenants in common." She drew up a list of restrictions: Henry cannot rent the house; he cannot cohabit there with a spouse; the house must be sold after three years; her share of the equity must then be put in trust for Cole. A month after her death, Henry is to be informed of this change.

Death is as close to her now as dreams are to sleep. Into these last fragile hours she has woven a fantasy of longed-for domestic peace and family happiness. On this last night they will be together. They will sit at table, her son on one side, her husband on the other. They will have dinner together, watch some television, kiss one another good-night. Saying goodbye to life, her ultimate joy is in the commonplace. This is her farewell gift to her son.

Late afternoon, Friday, February 11, 1994

It's been one crazy day for Nadine Porter, almost enough to grind her ebullient spirits down. Sue's been on edge for most of the week and now at the end of it has a dozen things she wants done. She's decided, for instance, that Oreo must have "the works"—brushing, shampoo, nail-clipping—and has asked Nadine to make an appointment at the dog salon for the following morning. She then decides that Gwynneth Powell, the night worker, who's coming on at four p.m., can make the call because she wants Nadine to pick up some new medication. Marilyn, the home nurse, has ordered a new supply of morphine and Ativan (a relaxant). The prescription is at the doctor's and has to be picked up and taken to the drugstore to be filled.

There's so much to do, however, that Sue changes her mind on this, too, and tells Nadine to forget it, not to worry. "There's plenty of time," she says, which surprises Nadine because Sue is usually adamant about ensuring her morphine supply.

The main thing is to get to the bank. Sue has already had Cole sign a savings account card once. Now she says his writing has improved so much, he should sign another one and she wants to go to the bank with him. It makes little sense to Nadine. It strikes her that fear is driving Sue: it's clear her ability to walk, to talk, is fading fast. Anyway, Nadine gets Sue out of the house and into the car where there's a portable wheelchair. They pick Cole up at his school and go to the bank in Sidney where he fills in another card.

After that, Sue seems satisfied, and when she's back home, Nadine helps her onto the stairwell glide, freshens her up and settles her down for a rest before dinner. She can hear Gwynneth come through the front door upstairs.

Sue now seems at peace. She's already decided they'll order dinner out that night and Nadine has got the menus from various restaurants and found out what Henry would like. So after she's turned on the "Oprah Winfrey Show," which Sue watches daily, she says a breezy good-bye. Sue can no longer turn her head toward the door but with effort responds: "I've been up all day. I'm very tired, shutting down. You have a good weekend."

Upstairs, Nadine tells Gwynneth about the dinner arrangements and asks her to make an appointment for Oreo the next morning. Then she takes off. Sue can't make up her mind what she'd like for dinner, mahi mahi mainly but a little pasta too. When Cole drops in, he says he'll order pasta and he and his mum can share.

After the night shift, Gwynneth usually leaves at eight a.m. but tomorrow she'll stay a couple of hours longer. Sue told her on Wednesday that a very special friend was coming Saturday for the day. If Gwynneth could stay just a couple of hours extra on Saturday morning, Sue said, there'd be no need for a home-maker to come in. Her friend could take care of her. Gwynneth agreed and the home-maker's shift for tomorrow has been canceled. Gwynneth feels a little curious about the identity of this "very special friend" but politeness precludes even the subtlest of queries. Now it's Friday night and Sue has still given no hint as to who it is, or even indicated whether it's a man or a woman.

When Gwynneth arrives back with the food, Sue suggests she set a place for herself and eat with them. Gwynneth usually has dinner after the family because Sue is so slow and Gwynneth's job is to feed her, so this invitation to eat along with the family is quite special. Henry's been in San Francisco during the week and brought back a fine bottle of white wine. When it's opened and the tall, thin glasses are filled, the atmosphere is festive, celebratory.

The meal is a memorable one. There's not only talk but laughter. Henry is loving and attentive, and Sue's speech, usually unintelligible by dinnertime, is understandable if one concentrates and guesses. She responds to Henry with light talk, wit and sparkle. There is a warmth and peace between them that Gwynneth has not seen before. She thinks, this is how it must have been with the two of them before the illness, before the breakup. Cole responds, gleefully posing some childish riddles, looking with laughter from one parent to the other while they struggle for the answer.

Every Friday night, this family has a little ritual. Cole is allowed to stay up with his parents an extra hour and they watch "Street Legal" together. Now usually, when Cole is going to bed at eight o'clock and comes in to say goodnight, Sue is being washed or having her teeth brushed. But this night when dinner is over and Sue and Gwynneth are downstairs, Sue says she doesn't want Cole to see her doing her toilet and she'd like to be sitting down when he arrives.

Gwynneth says okay and thinks nothing of it. But a strong impulse moves her when she hears Cole coming down the stairs. On instinct she sits Sue down on a low stool, stands behind her, and when Cole comes in, she gently moves Sue's arms, stiff and thin as sticks, enfolding them around Cole's slim body. The robot arms won't go high, but they reach around the small of the child's back. Sue gives her son a final embrace. The child, excited by the sheer happiness of the night, smiles at her. "Ah, Mum," he says, "you're being weird," and wiggles away.

A half hour before "Street Legal," Henry comes in and asks Sue if she'd like to get into the hot tub with them. He says, "I'll undress you, and lift you in." She says no, she's too tired, she's comfortable in bed and will stay there.

While Henry and Cole are in the tub, Gwynneth vacuums the upstairs of the house. This is not part of her duties but no one regularly cleans it. The house has become quite grubby, with the carpet spotted in part and anything out of arm's reach undusted. It is not the duty of the home-makers to clean. Sue dislikes a dirty house, so when Gwynneth tells her what she's done, Sue seems relieved, and Gwynneth knows that the mysterious visitor expected in the morning is the cause of her relief.

After Henry and Cole go to bed, Gwynneth gets Sue ready for the night. She changes the little booties Sue wears to protect her fleshless ankles and makes sure the protective pads are on her bony knees. Then she checks the foam padding which holds Sue's dislocated left shoulder in place. Sue remarks on how long it takes her to get ready and how exhausting the process is.

When Gwynneth turns out the light, it's nearly midnight.

Saturday, February 12, 1994

Sue rings for Gwynneth at five a.m. as usual to go to the bathroom and after that they both return to their beds, Gwynneth to sleep and Sue to quietly wait. At five to eight Gwynneth knocks on Sue's door and greets her as usual: "Good morning, Sunshine." Sue grins from her bed and asks the home-worker if she'd had any dreams that night, for Gwynneth often dreams and shares them with Sue.

"Sure did," said Gwynneth. "Of all things, I dreamed you were having a breathing attack. I ran around and found a little blue pill and gave it to you. And it saved your life."

Sue is silent for a moment and then says lightly: "Well, well, there she is! Cute as a button with her dreams."

This morning, Sue doesn't hesitate when she picks her clothes for the day. She doesn't seem to have thought about it: it's a spontaneous choice. She has two pairs of black spandex pants. "The old ones or the new ones?" Gwynneth asks. "Ah, let's see . . . the new ones, why not?" Sue says. She picks a blue denim shirt to go with them. The shirt is positively festive, a resort boutique item with pieces of multicolored glass scattered over the bodice, a fun, special-occasion shirt.

She drinks mint tea at breakfast, although she always has coffee, and when Gwynneth remarks that maybe she's excited about her friend coming, Sue looks at her and says very calmly: "I really am looking forward to it."

Sue then says that maybe she and her friend will go shopping. She mentions that Holly, the home-worker who is scheduled for that night, has been told not to come but to wait at her home until she hears from Sue or her friend. Because who knows? They might even decide to stay out for dinner.

Sue asks Gwynneth to pick out a pair of earrings. "Nothing too flashy," she says. Asked if she wants any makeup, Sue says no, just a little lipstick. But its color is too pale and Gwynneth is too gentle. "Come on," Sue says, "be a little assertive with that lipstick."

It is now 10 a.m. and time for Gwynneth to go. She calls out, "Bye, Cole, bye, Henry, see you in a few days." She waves to Sue who gives a faint smile.

On the threshold of the front door, Gwynneth hesitates. There are pieces of foam sewn into Sue's T-shirt, worn underneath, to protect her sore and jutting shoulder blades. They'd often joked about them. Sue would tell Gwynneth: "Be careful with those little bones because when it becomes time for me to fly away, that's where my wings will sprout from."

Sue is sitting in her wheelchair framed by the wide kitchen entranceway. As Gwynneth looks back, there is something about the way Sue is sitting, dressed up and expectant, that reminds Gwynneth of those "little wings." She hesitates, thinks of saying something, but decides against it. With a last wave, she goes flying out the door.

Gwynneth was sitting at home listening to music that night when the phone rang. A co-worker told her the news. She sat for some time, not wanting to move, trying to absorb it. It was 11 p.m. She thought of Henry and Cole. Too late to call. But just before midnight she called the house. Henry answered. He was very quiet. "Were you sleeping?" Gwynneth asked. No, he said, he was just lying there in the dark with Cole in his arms, the two of them awake and silent, hoping that the night would pass quickly.

Monday, February 14, 1994

At a press conference in Ottawa, a distraught Svend Robinson tells reporters that he was present when Sue Rodriguez died early Saturday afternoon. He had held her in his arms as she slipped into unconsciousness. She had died peacefully and with dignity. The only other person present, said Robinson, was an unnamed physician who had assisted Sue Rodriguez in taking her life. The Saturday date had been chosen in January. The only other person to know that Sue's death was planned for that day was her husband, Henry Rodriguez.

Tuesday, March 15, 1994

A pathologist's report reveals that Sue died of a massive overdose of morphine taken with Seconal capsules. The body, finally released by the police, has been cremated and the ashes given to her husband.

Epilogue

"She didn't particularly want to stay for Christmas and had planned to die in December. We had a long talk about it. I talked her out of it. I thought there was still more time and she should keep going. And she was concerned about the book, she wanted to make sure there'd be one. On the day, Henry stayed at a friend's, Cindy Ramsey, with Cole. Cole didn't know. Henry was supposed to call the house at four o'clock but he called at three. I told him Sue was dead. It took him some time to come as they had to pick up the dog, Oreo. When he came though the front door, he burst into tears. He and Cole went downstairs together. After a short while they came up, Cole holding Henry's hand. They had both been weeping but now were calm. In the evening, I gave Cole the letter that Sue had had written for him. I don't know whether he has heard the tape or not.

"Downstairs, Sue lay on her bed looking as if she were asleep. I had helped her onto it and had put a blanket over her. She was totally at peace, serene and ready when she took her dose. There was no doubt, no hesitation. She didn't think there'd be a band waiting for her on the other side. She just thought she'd be one with the elements and she was happy with that. I held her in my arms. She asked me to put a cassette on: she picked Deuter's 'Land of Enchantment.' It's a beautiful piece of music. Sue—these were her last words—said: 'Turn it down, it's too loud, I can't hear you talk.'"

Svend Robinson, April 2, 1994

Susan Jane Rodriguez
August 2, 1950—February 12, 1994

Birnie, Lisa Hobbs, 1928-
   Uncommon will : the death and life of Sue Rodriguez
/ Lisa Hobbs Birnie, Sue Rodriguez. -- Toronto :
Macmillan Canada, c1994.
   179 p. : ill.

07414722   ISBN:0771590911

1. Rodriguez, Sue, 1950-1994. 2. Amyotrophic
lateral sclerosis - Patients - Biography. 3. Right to die -
British Columbia. 4. Assisted suicide - British Columbia.
I. Rodriguez, Sue, 1950-1994. II. Title

2515   94JUL07   26/   1-01030455